Poor No More

Wealth Is Within Reach

CURTIS HILL

Certified Financial Planner™

MODERN MILLENNIUM PRESS
LOS ANGELES, CA

Copyright © 2008 Curtis Hill
All rights reserved.

Modern Millennium Press
Los Angeles, CA

ISBN: 1-4392-1256-2
ISBN-13: 9781439212561

Visit www.poor-no-more.com to order additional copies.

Certified Financial Planner Board of Standards Inc. owns the certification marks CFP®, CERTIFIED FINANCIAL PLANNER™ and federally registered CFP (with flame design) in the U.S which it awards to individuals who successfully complete CFP Board's initial and ongoing certification requirements

Special Thanks to My Friends that Helped Me Complete this Project:

John "Wesley" Davis

Jerry Persch

Ric Gaines

Patty Ellsworth

Dedication

This book is dedicated to my loving wife Irina for her infinite tolerance and patience while I was writing this book, and for giving me the endurance to complete this project.

Table of Contents

Chapter 1 – What's Really Behind Our Financial Decisions?	1
Chapter 2 – Sixty-Five Is Not a Magic Number	9
Chapter 3 – The Goal Is Financial Freedom, Not Retirement	19
Chapter 4 – Freedom Account Dynamics	29
Chapter 5 – Madison Avenue Versus Us	43
Chapter 6 – Our "NEEDS" Versus Our "WANTS"	51
Chapter 7 – Planning and Budgeting	57
Chapter 8 – Living Well on Less	67
Chapter 9 – Debt Is a Four-Letter Word	87
Chapter 10 – Cars: Budget Sucking Machines	99
Chapter 11 – You Versus Car Dealerships	109
Chapter 12 – How Did I Blow All That	123
Chapter 13 – Proper Use and Control of Credit	129
Chapter 14 – Home Sweet Mortgage	149
Chapter 15 – The Power of Compounding (Are We Getting Ahead?)	169
Chapter 16 – Investments Aren't Mysterious	183
Chapter 17 – Untrue Investment Truisms or the Effects of Aiming Too Low	203
Chapter 18 – Wrapping It All Up	221

Chapter 1
What's Really Behind Our Financial Decisions?

It had been a long day. My head was thumping with a splitting headache. Since my office was over a pharmacy, I went downstairs to buy some Advil™. Two hours later, with my head cleared from the pain, I asked myself, "Why Advil™?" My purchase had been spontaneous, without thought. Who had placed the idea in my head that Advil™ was the solution? Would not the store brand's ibuprofen have been just as good at half the price? Why did I buy Advil™? Do I exercise control over my other purchases and financial decisions?

My premise is that we no longer properly exercise choice or free will when it comes to our financial decisions. In fact, these decisions are becoming increasingly involuntary, without our conscious control. We have been promoted to, advertised to, marketed to, and sold to so often that we can no longer think for ourselves. When it comes to personal financial decisions, our minds have become cluttered with so much external self-serving advice and clever product advertisements that outside influences have taken control of our financial "belief system."

Do our beliefs betray us? Are we aware of the sources of our beliefs? Are our beliefs controlled by others?

So what does our belief system have to do with money and finance? It's simple; we make our daily decisions based on what we "believe" is good or bad, what we "believe" is desirable or not, what we "believe" we deserve or not, what we "believe" we need or not, and what we "believe" we can afford or not. Most of our decision-making processes begin with our belief system. That is why the source of our beliefs is so critical. My question to the reader is: Have we considered where our beliefs come from? Wise people should be suspicious of the source of their beliefs, and should be aware of how and why these beliefs became part of their psyche.

If freedom is defined by having control, how can we have freedom if we give up control of our belief system to outside forces that have self-serving motives?

When we consider the sheer volume of advertising and marketing we encounter, it is self-evident that our financial belief system has been corrupted by sinister outside forces. These outside forces have their own agendas that seldom align with our best interests. These forces consider only their own goals - corporate profits. Corporate marketing has become so effective that it can implant ideas and concepts within our financial belief system without our knowledge. These corrupted concepts, implanted within our financial belief system, are toxic to our monetary well-being.

Please note that I do not intend to beat up corporations. They are only doing what I, as a stockholder, would insist they do: attempting to maximize sales and profits. I just want the reader to be aware that corporate profit motives may conflict with our personal best interests.

Don't let corporations brainwash us and control our beliefs!

As consumers and as stewards of our own financial well-being, we have become brainwashed. We need to take more responsibility for our financial lives. We need to regain control! Madison Avenue advertising executives make our daily financial decisions for us without our knowledge or objections. We continue to make daily monetary decisions using our corrupted financial belief system, which causes us to remain dependent on our paychecks. Our financial ruin is certain unless we can regain control.

A popular health craze is to use various cleansing regimens to remove the toxins from our bodies. Similarly, we need to cleanse our minds of financial concepts and beliefs that were placed there by sinister outside forces with their own financial agendas. This book endeavors to identify and debunk these inappropriate beliefs, and will recommend regimens to recognize and cleanse inappropriate financial beliefs from our psyches. This book also provides tools to help us make appropriate financial, purchasing, and living decisions. The goal is a better life, without monetary pressures and free from outside malicious financial interference. The goal is financial freedom.

Do we think for ourselves? Or are we sheep following the herd?

Financially we have become sheep, following everyone else, unable to think for ourselves. It is easy to believe that being in debt is normal when everyone around us is in debt. We find comfort in being like everyone else we know. It is easy and convenient to not question our financial beliefs or where they came from. We accept our financial beliefs as fact even though these beliefs are implanted by outside forces. Therefore, our attitudes about what we spend money on, how much debt we take on, how we should work, how we should retire, when we should retire, and what we can expect to achieve in our lives is largely controlled by massive corporate advertising campaigns.

Corporations have trained us to desire their products regardless of our ability to afford them. Then, these corporations provide us with credit to enslave us with the chains of debt. In the end, we are left wanting more than we have and without the funds to buy what we really need. Our desires, implanted within us by outside forces, have taken control of us.

Who controls our purchases: Madison Avenue or us?

So how do we shatter the chains of debt and break our addictions to purchasing items we don't need? How do we block sinister outside influences? How do we plan for the future? How do we retake control of our lives? People attempt to do so by reading financial self-help books and by seeking the advice of financial planners.

Reading self-help books is a good idea because, at a minimum, this exercise encourages self-reflection about the financial decisions we are making. However, please remember that most self-help books are designed to sell more books by promising easy solutions. Authors can sell more books if they offer solutions that are simple to understand and require little change. Thus, I have not found a financial self-help book that addresses core belief issues. Without correcting our corrupted financial beliefs, it would be difficult to achieve financial freedom. This book focuses on workable practical solutions to our financial issues that will lead to financial freedom.

Financial planners can also be helpful. However, they are typically compensated by the collections of assets under the planner's management. This creates a potential conflict of interest. The planner's recommended solutions are often geared around the long-term collection of assets for future needs such as retirement, children's educations, major purchases, estate planning, etc. It is contrary to the planner's own pay incentives to encourage investors to spend and enjoy their assets. Thus, many financial planners may place the quality of their clients' current lifestyles on the back burner. Further, many financial planners embrace some of the corrupted financial beliefs that limit our concepts of what is possible, practical, and achievable. In short, we need to learn how to think for ourselves.

Most financial books and planners focus on retirement planning issues instead of more important current lifestyle issues.

The objective of many personal financial books and financial planners is to teach us how to manage our assets and debt so that we can build wealth to eventually retire, as though retirement should be our main goal. Typically these books and planners define "financial independence" as the ability to retire. Retirement should not be our main or only goal. I believe that focusing primarily on retirement falls short of what is achievable and desirable. Financial books and financial planners focus primarily on retirement planning instead of lifestyle issues. This narrow focus contributes to the corruption of our belief system by limiting our perception of what is achievable through good financial management.

Thus, seeking outside help can result in further "belief" manipulation. If we recognize when and how we are being manipulated, we can break free of the chains that restrict us and learn how to think for ourselves. True financial freedom becomes achievable only when we remove the control and influence of outside forces. Proper outside advice should *not* tell us what we should do. Proper outside advice should only give us the appropriate tools to evaluate and make our own decisions.

True financial freedom is more than just financial independence. It is the power to choose and think for ourselves without personal monetary pressures or outside influence.

Many financial books and planners focus on collecting assets and guiding our investments. Although their advice can be very useful, it is of no value if we don't have the money to invest. How do we obtain the free cash to invest when we can't make ends meet? Many self-help books recommend "get rich quick" schemes that sometimes even suggest taking on more debt in order to make our fortunes. These schemes are ridiculous, risky, and often result in financial ruin. This book will coach its readers on how to find and enjoy the money they already have but are wasting, and how to find the money to change their lives.

Wealth comes from one thing, and that thing is the ability to make good decisions in our lives. Regardless of our income level, wealth will be fleeting unless we make good financial decisions. However, few of us are trained to make these decisions, and many outside forces, through advertising, are encouraging us to make bad monetary choices. This book is all about improving our financial decisions and about regaining control of our lives.

This book will demonstrate techniques to obtain financial independence early in life. Further, this goal can be achieved without high risk, debt, risky stock investment, over leveraged real estate, or other "get rich quick" schemes. The key to reaching this goal is cleansing our thoughts from corrupted financial beliefs that hold us back.

Chapter Takeaway
Our financial decision-making process is greatly influenced by our core financial belief system. However, this belief system has been highly contaminated by years of advertising and marketing. One of the differences between wealthy and poor people is that the wealthy have learned to identify corrupting financial influences and how to neutralize their disruptive

effects on their lives. In short, they have learned how to think for themselves.

Just as a farmer must clear the weeds and rocks from a field before he can plow and plant, we must identify and remove the massive number of inappropriate money-related ideas in our heads. Just like the farmer preparing his field to be planted, we must prepare our heads by removing unsuitable financial habits and then relearn how to think about money.

We can never be wealthy if we still think like a poor person.

Chapter 2
Sixty-Five Is Not a Magic Number

Outside forces manipulate more than our purchase decisions; they also manipulate our beliefs about retirement. Our corrupted beliefs about retirement often conflict with our true retirement desires. Many people believe they should stop working in a career they enjoy at age sixty-five, or whatever the standard retirement age is for their industry. Others believe they should continue working in a career they hate until age sixty-five. What is magical about age sixty-five or any other predefined retirement age? Why can't we work longer if we enjoy our careers? Conversely, why should we work one single day longer in a career we loathe? We spend far too little time contemplating these important questions because many of us simply believe that a predefined retirement age is normal and that we should do what is normal. Let's discard our preprogrammed beliefs about retirement. Let's thaw out our frozen dreams about how life should be and make these dreams our new retirement plan!

Retirement is an obsolete concept!

From a corporate viewpoint, retirement is a tool that allows corporations to easily dispose of us when they are done with us – and not before. Corporations are not interested in our post-retirement contentment. They see normal retirement age as the point where it is more economical for the company to replace our greater experience and higher salary with younger, more energetic, and lower-paid employees.

From an individual's viewpoint, retirement is an obsolete concept that presumes we wish to spend all our time fishing, playing golf, or indulging in other leisure activities. The concept falsely assumes we will all be less active as we reach retirement age. Today's retirees are more active and do more than just participate in leisure activities. The concept also falsely assumes that it is reasonable to delay our dreams and goals until retirement. We should decide when we leave the corporate world, rather than the corporation deciding for us. We should not be influenced by what others think is normal or expected.

We should forget about the whole concept of "retirement." Instead, we should focus on obtaining a wider goal: financial freedom. We can achieve our dreams much earlier if we are prepared to take a different path from what society normally dictates to us.

The goal should not be retirement at age sixty-five, but instead thawing out our frozen dreams as soon as possible.

Let me give a real-life example. An acquaintance of mine - let's call him Fred - had worked as an engineer for a phone company all his life. Due to impending layoffs, he was offered an early retirement package at age fifty-five. He took the retirement package because it gave him the cash to start the business he had been dreaming about.

Fred wanted to design test equipment that would simplify his previous job. Now free from his employment, he had the spare time to design this equipment. He found junior partners happy to exchange their design expertise for a percentage in the new company. He used some of his own money and raised some seed money from friends and former co-workers who believed in him. Fred used the money to hire a few engineers and to build a prototype. The launch of Fred's new product was a great success.

To cut to the chase, after only three years and incredible growth of his startup company, Fred decided to sell his business to a much larger test equipment company that could better handle the growing demand. With several million dollars in his pocket and, more important, the satisfying feeling of personal success, Fred now looked forward to spending more time with his family. At this point, he entered his second early retirement and his workshop to enjoy building wooden toys for his grandchildren.

Cutting to the chase again, three years later, Fred sold his highly successful toy company to a much larger toy company for another multimillion-dollar check!

It was at about this time when Fred confided to me, "Retirement just doesn't seem to work for me." He went on to say, "I keep finding things that excite me enough that I just enjoy pursuing the idea with passion. I don't have time for retirement. I just wish I had started this earlier!"

It then occurred to me that Fred was enjoying his retirement to its fullest but did not realize it. This was because he had a different concept about what retirement should be. He incorrectly thought that retirement would be all about leisure. It is clear from Fred's example that we should reexamine and redefine our personal retirement goals. This is the time in our lives to thaw out our frozen dreams. Traditional retirement is an obsolete concept, long overdue to be replaced by a newer concept of being able to do what we enjoy. We never need to retire from doing what we love and enjoy.

For Fred, enjoyable retirement was all about pursuing new ideas and concepts. Building companies is Fred's equivalent to completing crossword puzzles or golfing. To Fred, starting new companies is fun and enjoyable. Therefore, these pursuits are the right "retirement" activities for Fred. But, as Fred stated, "I should have done this earlier." Fred would have been able to indulge his "retirement" activities (starting new companies) much earlier if he did not need his paycheck. This book and its financial freedom account concept are all about having the money to pursue our dreams earlier.

What are the right activities for us? Let's open our minds to the possibilities. Let's redefine retirement as the ability and freedom to chase our dreams.

Retirement is not an age! It is a lifestyle free to pursue our desires without financial burdens.

Why do so many people believe the proper retirement age is around sixty-five? What is magical about this age? Would it be irresponsible or unrealistic for someone entering the workforce today to dream of retiring at the age of only thirty-five, forty, or forty-five? To answer these questions, let's examine how corporate America, government, and even society as a whole have corrupted our belief system about retirement and success.

Corporations have duped us into believing that we should remain dependent on our paychecks until retirement age.

At the turn of the twentieth century, the vast majority of people in the United States owned their own businesses, i.e., mostly family farms and stores. Thinking independently was a way of life in that era because we needed to do so in order to run our own businesses.

At the turn of the twenty-first century, the majority of people worked for corporations. Corporations tell us what to do at work. After work, mass marketing and advertising campaigns tell us what to do, what to think, how to vote, what to desire, how to buy it, where to buy it, and what we should expect out of life in the future. We have gotten out of the habit of thinking for ourselves. As an example, we believe we should continue to work until retirement age. Many of us just accept this belief without further questions. This is another corrupt concept in our belief system.

Most people feel that financial security comes in the form of a corporate paycheck. Who placed this corrupted belief into our psyches?

Most people cannot imagine that it is practical to work for themselves instead of a corporation. Many feel it is more responsible, safe, and secure to work for a large corporation.

Corporations encourage and perpetuate these feelings. Further, most corporations set their retirement and pension plans around a "normal" retirement age of sixty-five. After all, it is in the corporations' best interests to keep us working for them as long as we are productive.

Corporations have no natural interest in teaching us how to become financially independent. They naturally need us to remain dependent on our paychecks. I don't intend to bash corporations; I just want my readers to understand their obvious motives. They don't teach methods or provide a path for early retirement. They tend to match only the first few percentage points we place in a 401(k) plan, thus encouraging us to minimize our retirement savings. They tend to encourage debt and even allow borrowing against their retirement plans.

When social security began, in the 1930's depression era, the retirement age of sixty-two was established for a different reason. The government wanted to push older people out of the job market earlier to create more jobs for younger, unemployed people. However, due to the enormous influence corporations have over government policy, the original intent of trying to get people to retire earlier has been perverted into penalizing people who want to end their employment earlier.

Social security benefits and retirement tax laws are structured to penalize us for early retirement.

Government policy conspires with corporate goals by further supporting this age sixty-five retirement standard. As evidence, the law provides that full social security benefits are paid only at age sixty-five or later. If we were born after 1960, this age becomes sixty-eight. No benefits are paid before age sixty-two. The government fosters the belief in an older retirement age by penalizing early withdrawals from IRAs, pension plans, and annuities before age fifty-nine and a half. These rules have the effect of telling the public that it is irresponsible to retire early, and that the government will not assist our early retirement. Finally, these rules corrupt our belief system by emphasizing that financial independence from our jobs is achievable only later in our lives. Thus the government's rules also encourage us to remain dependent on our paychecks.

High school programs include basic personal health education. Why don't they also include basic personal financial education?

It would seem logical that a government, wanting its people to prosper, would offer education on personal financial management and independence. However, when was the last time we went to a government-sponsored event promoting financial independence? Our high schools typically provide only minimal training on personal budgeting, managing our credit scores, managing our investments, or even balancing our checkbooks. The government just isn't in the business of promoting personal financial independence. This would be contrary to the corporate goal of keeping us dependent on our paychecks.

We should not expect our friends to embrace our new independence goals.

Society rejects people and concepts that are different and instead promotes homogeneity. If we are financially independent at age forty and most other people must wait until age sixty-five, society must either accept that we are smarter and better or reject us as being too different. Don't count on society accepting that we are smarter and better.

When we move forward financially, less secure friends might feel both jealous and threatened at first. Let's not worry though; they will adjust and become proud to know us. Plus, we will be adding new friends who are also successful, dynamic, and interesting as we move forward.

Chapter Takeaway

Our attitudes about retirement are core beliefs placed in us by outside forces that may not have our best interests at heart. Further, when it comes to money and retirement, most people haven't examined what they believe or why they believe it. Rather, they simply accept their core beliefs about retirement without ever questioning them. As a result, most people accept unthinkingly that early retirement and/or early financial independence is not a reasonable goal.

However, as I have said before, retirement is an obsolete concept. Instead of saving for retirement, we should save for the financial independence required to pursue our dreams. The financial freedom account concept introduced later in this book shows how we can obtain our dreams earlier.

This book will illustrate techniques to make early financial independence a reasonable and attainable goal. Further, this goal can be achieved without high risk, debt, risky stock investment, over leveraged real estate, or other "get rich quick" schemes. Instead, this goal can be reached with simple, sound financial management and an uncorrupted financial belief system.

Chapter 3
The Goal Is Financial Freedom, Not Retirement

Anyone can achieve financial success. However, most conventional solutions to achieving this success require hard work, many years of savings, and many types of lifestyle sacrifices. A lot of people buy into this hard-work conventional solution to financial success, and they sacrifice much of their personal lifestyles to accomplish monetary success. At the other extreme, many others focus on personal lifestyle and sacrifice financial success. Which are you, a workaholic or a playaholic? What can we do to find the golden measure, that happy medium, between the two?

Workaholics
We all know people who work over sixty hours a week to provide for themselves and/or the family that they seldom see. These workaholics may drive nice cars to their nice houses, all supported by high debt loads. These workaholics' high incomes qualify them for their luxury homes and cars. However, this just turns these workaholics into slaves to their higher-paying jobs and debt loads. Health issues or job layoffs can bring their lifestyles crashing down, like a fragile house of cards.

The typical workaholic has little room for error. If anything goes wrong, their high debts can cause their whole over-leveraged lifestyles to collapse. Workaholics accept this high risk because they believe they need their expensive status symbols. They believe that a higher income to support their lifestyles is just around the corner. Workaholics' lifestyles are often based on delayed satisfaction. They believe that all will be better when they get that next credential or promotion. Their belief system has been corrupted into thinking this is normal. To them, living within their means and with financial serenity is something they will only have in the future, after that next promotion.

My question is: Who wants this? Where is the quality of life? Who programmed our corrupted belief system to make us think that this workaholic lifestyle is acceptable? I argue that it is possible to achieve substantial financial success through better personal financial management and less personal lifestyle sacrifice.

Playaholics

Other people have no plan for achieving financial success. They live for the present, with little thought of the future. These playaholics tend to have lots of toys, boats, motorcycles, musical instruments, etc. They live hand to mouth. Rather than planning and budgeting, these people allow their purchase decisions to be driven by their loan companies' qualification criteria. They transfer their budgeting and financial decisions to the salesman or his finance guy. They don't seem to realize that just because we can qualify for a purchase does not mean we can afford to make the purchase. Obviously, with no plan for financial success, these playaholics will not achieve financial freedom.

Common Issues

Both workaholics and playaholics tend to be over-leveraged, with too much debt. Both tend to dangerously rely on uninterrupted employment. Both tend to put too little, if any, away for future needs or, as I prefer to say, "financial freedom." Both tend to falsely believe that putting 10% of their incomes into their 401(k) plans (if that much) is all the financial planning they need to do.

During the days of ancient Roman and Egyptian empires, slavery was the natural consequence of a weak nation being conquered by one of the imperial armies. The modern-day equivalent of these Roman legions is the massive corporate advertising campaigns that conquer and enslave our weak minds. Their clever marketing campaigns convince us to purchase items we don't need and to use debt to complete these purchases. Thus, we become slaves to servicing our debt loads. With high debt payments, we are only a few missed paychecks away from financial ruin. Therefore, we must ensure low risk with our employment situations. Keeping our jobs becomes a priority, and thus we become slaves to our employers. Why do we feel the need to enslave ourselves with debt?

Sue had just moved to Los Angeles and was scraping to get by. She needed a car in order to get around town. Although it took her several months, she finally secured a decent job. The day she obtained the job offer, she returned to her apartment building in a brand-new BMW 3 Series. At this point, she certainly qualified to lease the new vehicle, but did she really need a BMW? Did she feel pressure to "keep up with the Joneses"? Sue had just gotten herself out of unemployment. Why did she feel the need to put herself back in a financial bind with debt? It is the corruption of our belief system that forces us to make these irrational purchase decisions. We need to think for ourselves and recognize when marketing executives have their hands in our wallets.

Why do workaholics and playaholics allow themselves to become so dependent on their next paycheck? Like most financial problems, it starts with a corrupted belief system. In this case, both groups tend to incorrectly believe they have a social contract with their employers. They believe that their "contract" provides steady lifelong employment leading to guaranteed retirement. They incorrectly believe their work situation is permanent. This womb-to-tomb concept may have worked for our grandfathers and maybe even for our fathers. However, it is unlikely to work for us. Corporations are happy to dump us as soon as a lower-cost provider can replace our skill set, leaving us unprepared for the job market. Consider all the jobs that have been outsourced to China and India over the past few years. We must take responsibility for and ownership of planning our own future.

Most people are just not prepared to do this planning. So they may consult a financial advisor or financial planner for help. The problem with this is that most financial planners have bought into the traditional concept of a modest retirement at a traditional retirement age. This traditional concept falls far short of what is possible and achievable.

Most financial planners and investment advisors believe the primary goal of their clients is preparing for retirement. Therefore, it's no wonder that so few people start this process at an early age. Is it practical or reasonable to expect a twenty-one-year-old entering the work force to be concerned about retirement when that event is many decades away?

However, the same twenty-one-year-old would be interested in a plan that allowed him to travel, ski, or surf without limit and without worry about his paychecks, particularly if this is achievable by age thirty-five. One of the problems with conventional financial planning is that the goals are set too low. How can any young person be interested in traditional planning for the future when the results are so mediocre and so many years away?

To achieve financial freedom early in life without substantial lifestyle sacrifices requires an unconventional approach. Many people have trouble with this because they are uncomfortable being unconventional or different from their friends. The need to conform overrides their desires for financial freedom. However, if I can demonstrate a way to achieve this freedom quickly and with few real lifestyle sacrifices, perhaps everyone will break from conformity and adopt a plan for a better future.

People often have an inaccurate concept of retirement; they believe that people suddenly stop working forever the day they retire. While this is sometimes true, studies indicate that most retirees are working again within one year of retirement. While inadequate retirement resources sometimes cause this, more often it is because retirees are entertained by their new careers.

For example, an old surfer might open a surf shop because he really enjoys talking to surfers all day.

Retirement should be defined as doing whatever we enjoy without worrying about a paycheck or the boss's wishes. Retirement is not an age. It is a state of mind that begins with financial serenity.

Problematically, many people view retirement as the day they switch from living off their paychecks to living off retirement investments. Believing that this dramatic change can come so easily so late in our lives is a fallacy.

Learning how to manage an income portfolio and how to live within its limits takes years. Are we better drivers now than the first day we started driving? Of course, driving well takes time and practice. Similarly, it takes time to learn how to manage our investments and become comfortable doing so. Learning to live off investment income should be a gradual process rather than an abrupt change late in life. In later chapters, this book will touch on some investment basics.

For many people, living off investment income is unnatural. They feel that living off a paycheck is more natural, despite the fact that investment income is more reliable than a paycheck that is subject to a boss's whims. Thus, learning to rely on investment income is difficult for some people.

However, changes are easier to accept and adapt to if made gradually. We need to progressively become more dependent on investment income and less dependent on our paychecks.

As this change is occurring, we are also approaching financial freedom.

Freedom Account

Now I wish to introduce a major concept. Don't save for retirement in the conventional sense. Instead, place money in what I call a freedom account. A freedom account differs from a conventional retirement account in two major ways:

1) <u>Why</u> we are building this account.
2) <u>When</u> we start withdrawing from this account.

We should start withdrawing money from this account in the second year. The size of these withdrawals should grow every year as we become more dependent on our freedom accounts and less dependent on our paychecks. As we become less dependent on our paychecks (due to our growing withdrawals from our freedom accounts), we are able to contribute a larger percentage of our paychecks each year to these accounts.

What I am describing here is a cascade effect that makes early financial independence possible. I understand that the concept and the math involved in the above statement may seem a little fuzzy or at least unconventional to many. However, I will demonstrate in the following chapters that the concept will work with ease.

This may seem like a shell game - i.e., it may appear that we are moving money around for no reason. In fact, there is a method to this strategy. We are progressively learning to depend on our investment income. Furthermore, we are gradually decreasing our dependence on our paychecks. Reducing dependence on our paychecks equates to financial freedom.

The most important, yet unconventional, concept about the freedom account is that its benefits are near-term. Unlike the distant benefits of a classic retirement account, benefits from our freedom accounts begin flowing in the second year. This is one of the reasons why a twenty-one-year-old can buy into this concept.

It's easier to place money in an account we can benefit from next year than a classic retirement account whose benefits are decades away!

The freedom account gradually trains us to live off our investment assets instead of our paychecks. The process of weaning us off our paychecks starts in year two and quickly accelerates. This decreasing dependence on our paychecks brings with it a positive change in the outlook about our finances. Further, it brings what I call "financial serenity."

The goal of the freedom account is to establish financial serenity, which renders obsolete the need for retirement planning. Further, this can be achieved in fifteen to twenty years instead of the forty-five-year path of conventional retirement!

An additional significant benefit of the freedom account is that it enables people to take career risks. Many people are so dependent on their regular paychecks that they may turn down better-paying jobs, self-employment opportunities, or commission-related career paths in favor of their current steady paychecks. These people are trapped in their lower-paying and less-satisfying jobs because they can't afford a career misstep since financial disaster is only a few missed paychecks away.

However, as our freedom accounts grow, we should become less dependent on our paychecks and more able to accept riskier higher-paying opportunities. This possibility of advancing our financial independence is enabled by the safety net our freedom accounts provide.

My father once told me that most people work hard for their money while wealthy people relax and let their money work hard for them. This book is all about making the latter situation a reality for all of us!

Chapter Takeaway

Most people are over-leveraged with debt due to overspending on status symbols and toys. These people are getting into a trap set up by their high debt loads. Missing just a few paychecks can cause financial ruin. Thus, they are over-dependent on their current jobs. They cannot afford to take any career risk that might result in higher income. They must instead opt for job security. This leaves them trapped in this unfulfilling career situation until traditional retirement age.

Saving for later seems unimportant when the traditional concept of retirement is multiple decades away. Instant gratification becomes more important. However, my concept of a freedom account results in benefits starting the very next year. Thus, saving can have near-term benefits. This concept teaches us how to gain financial independence over only a few years and allows us to take the risk of that higher-paying career path. This concept also replaces the need for retirement planning, as we will have already become accustomed to living off our investments long before we reach traditional retirement age.

Chapter 4
Freedom Account Dynamics

It is common to save 10% to 15% of our incomes toward retirement or other future needs. These savings are often directed to our 401(k) plans. With proper financial management, most individuals can increase their savings to 20% or more. Further, by embracing the freedom account concept, we can reduce our dependency on our paychecks and learn to live on investment income.

Twenty percent may seem like a high, if not impossible, level of savings. Don't worry; this book will demonstrate ways to increase our savings while improving our lifestyles. We all have friends who live as well as we do while making only 80% of our income. In fact, I bet we all know someone who makes only 60% of our income whose lifestyle is similar to our own. My point is that saving more is possible and can be accomplished without lifestyle sacrifices.

Many people live hand to mouth. They spend every dime they make every month.

By applying proper financial management skills and improving our spending decisions, we can find ways to save 20% of our income. I am *not* suggesting that we make major sacrifices to make this possible. In fact, I believe we can increase savings while improving our lifestyles. The key is learning to think for ourselves instead of letting Madison Avenue advertising executives make our purchasing decisions. This book will focus on ways to do this without diminishing our current lifestyles.

Again, I am *not* proposing additional savings at the expense of lifestyle sacrifices. Most people truly waste more than 20% of their income. With the help of the tools and techniques suggested in this book, we can learn how to identify and take back this waste. Recapturing this wasted money won't diminish our lifestyles. In fact, our lifestyles will improve as we gain financial serenity.

To recapture waste, we must cleanse our minds of the corrupted financial beliefs that have been programmed by the sinister outside forces of advertising and marketing agencies I mentioned previously. These corrupted beliefs cause us to waste money by allowing outside marketing forces, instead of ourselves, to direct our expenditures. We cannot achieve financial freedom until we take back control of our beliefs. Only then we can cut the waste and learn to increase our savings.

We can use the recaptured waste to increase our savings; this becomes the basis of our freedom accounts. The effect of compounding this additional savings is incredible. In addition, we will be training ourselves to live off the investment income from our freedom accounts instead of our employment income. When all our living expenses are funded by our freedom accounts, we have achieved financial freedom.

The freedom account concept differs from traditional savings or retirement accounts in several ways:

1) We learn to trust that our investment income will pay our living expenses.
2) We learn to view employment income as only a vehicle to expand our freedom accounts and thus our independence.
3) We start making withdrawals in the second year and increase them each year.
4) Our contribution rate increases each year.

We should begin by saving 20% of our income in our freedom accounts. Increase this by 5% each year. Some of you may be asking, "I could barely afford to save 20%. How could I possibly save more each year?" The answer is simple: Income from our freedom accounts increasingly replaces our employment income, thus allowing us to save more. Now that I've made it really confusing, let me give an example.

Each year we save more in our freedom accounts. If we increase by 5% a year, this would mean our savings rate will start at 20%, then go up to 25% the second year, and 30% the third year, and continuing until all of our employment income goes to our freedom accounts.

We can afford to invest the extra 5% each year because we will also be withdrawing an increasing 5% each year from our freedom accounts. In year two, we will withdraw the equivalent of 5% of our employment income from our freedom accounts. This withdrawal will grow to 10% in the third year, 15% in the fourth year, and will continue to grow at 5% per year. This withdrawal from our freedom accounts supplements our current income and allows our savings rate to grow. Our effective net savings rate continues at 20%, where effective net saving is defined as the difference between the total amount of employment income we save, less the amount we withdraw from our freedom accounts. As an example, if we save 50% of our income in our freedom accounts and withdraw 30% from our freedom accounts, our effective savings rate remains at 20%. Again, we are learning to live off our freedom accounts rather than our employment income. *See Table 4.1.*

Let me explain the same example again in a different way. In year one, we invest 20% of our employment income into our freedom accounts. In year two, we invest 25% of our income into our freedom accounts and supplement our living income by withdrawing the equivalent of 5% of our employment income out of our freedom accounts. In year three, we invest 30% of our income into our freedom accounts and supplement our living income by withdrawing the equivalent of 10% of our employment income out of our freedom accounts.

Continuing this approach, in year sixteen we invest 95% of our employment income into our freedom accounts and supplement our living income by withdrawing the equivalent of 75% of our employment income out of our freedom accounts. In the seventeenth and all subsequent years, we invest 100% of our employment income into our freedom accounts and supplement our living income by withdrawing the equivalent of 80% of our employment income out of our freedom accounts. Beginning in the seventeenth year, we are living completely off our freedom accounts. The purpose of continuing our employment is to add to our freedom accounts and increase our financial independence. *See Table 4.1.*

Table 4.1
Freedom Account Dynamics
Independence Growing at 5% with 20% Start

Year	After-Tax Income	Percent Contribution to Freedom Account	Cash Contribution to Freedom Account	10% Interest on Prior Year Ending Balance	Percent Withdrawal for Current Year Support	Cash Withdrawal for Current Year Support	Freedom Account Year Ending Balance
1	$100,000	20.0%	$20,000	$0	0.0%	$0	$20,000
2	$100,000	25.0%	$25,000	$2,000	5.0%	-$5,000	$42,000
3	$100,000	30.0%	$30,000	$4,200	10.0%	-$10,000	$66,200
4	$100,000	35.0%	$35,000	$6,620	15.0%	-$15,000	$92,820
5	$100,000	40.0%	$40,000	$9,282	20.0%	-$20,000	$122,102
6	$100,000	45.0%	$45,000	$12,210	25.0%	-$25,000	$154,312
7	$100,000	50.0%	$50,000	$15,431	30.0%	-$30,000	$189,743
8	$100,000	55.0%	$55,000	$18,974	35.0%	-$35,000	$228,718
9	$100,000	60.0%	$60,000	$22,872	40.0%	-$40,000	$271,590
10	$100,000	65.0%	$65,000	$27,159	45.0%	-$45,000	$318,748
11	$100,000	70.0%	$70,000	$31,875	50.0%	-$50,000	$370,623
12	$100,000	75.0%	$75,000	$37,062	55.0%	-$55,000	$427,686
13	$100,000	80.0%	$80,000	$42,769	60.0%	-$60,000	$490,454
14	$100,000	85.0%	$85,000	$49,045	65.0%	-$65,000	$559,500
15	$100,000	90.0%	$90,000	$55,950	70.0%	-$70,000	$635,450
16	$100,000	95.0%	$95,000	$63,545	75.0%	-$75,000	$718,995
17	$100,000	100.0%	$100,000	$71,899	80.0%	-$80,000	$810,894
18	$100,000	100.0%	$100,000	$81,089	80.0%	-$80,000	$911,983
19	$100,000	100.0%	$100,000	$91,198	80.0%	-$80,000	$1,023,182
20	$100,000	100.0%	$100,000	$102,318	80.0%	-$80,000	$1,145,500
21	$100,000	100.0%	$100,000	$114,550	80.0%	-$80,000	$1,280,050
22	$100,000	100.0%	$100,000	$128,005	80.0%	-$80,000	$1,428,055
23	$100,000	100.0%	$100,000	$142,805	80.0%	-$80,000	$1,590,860
24	$100,000	100.0%	$100,000	$159,086	80.0%	-$80,000	$1,769,947
25	$100,000	100.0%	$100,000	$176,995	80.0%	-$80,000	$1,966,941
26	$100,000	100.0%	$100,000	$196,694	80.0%	-$80,000	$2,183,635
27	$100,000	100.0%	$100,000	$218,364	80.0%	-$80,000	$2,421,999
28	$100,000	100.0%	$100,000	$242,200	80.0%	-$80,000	$2,684,199
29	$100,000	100.0%	$100,000	$268,420	80.0%	-$80,000	$2,972,619
30	$100,000	100.0%	$100,000	$297,262	80.0%	-$80,000	$3,289,880
31	$100,000	100.0%	$100,000	$328,988	80.0%	-$80,000	$3,638,868
32	$100,000	100.0%	$100,000	$363,887	80.0%	-$80,000	$4,022,755
33	$100,000	100.0%	$100,000	$402,276	80.0%	-$80,000	$4,445,031
34	$100,000	100.0%	$100,000	$444,503	80.0%	-$80,000	$4,909,534
35	$100,000	100.0%	$100,000	$490,953	80.0%	-$80,000	$5,420,487

With the above example, we have effectively saved 20% per year. More importantly, we've learned how to live off and manage our investments. After year sixteen, we are no longer working to pay the bills, and instead all of our income goes toward improving our independence, and all of our living expenses come from withdrawals from our freedom accounts.

We have achieved our goal. Our money is working for us instead of us working for money.

This doesn't mean that we can suddenly stop working and go fishing, that is, fall into the old concept of retirement. We still may not have enough in our freedom accounts to support us for the remainder of our lives and the interest income from our freedom account may not yet support all our withdrawals. However, it does mean we can look at our career choices differently as we become more independent. In chapters 2 and 3, we redefined the old concept of "age sixty-five retirement" into a more practical goal of independence and financial serenity at an earlier age. Building a fat freedom account provides for this financial freedom.

The reasonable question is: Why play the shell game of moving money in and out of the freedom account? The answer: It's nearly impossible to suddenly switch from living off our employment income to living off our investment income. This sudden change often results in disastrous retirement mismanagement for some unlucky people. It takes time to learn how to manage our investment accounts and time to trust that our investment income is reliable.

Switching from living off employment income to living off investment income should be a slow, gradual process.

In the above example, the investment into the freedom account started at 20% of our employment income. Each subsequent year we grew our independence by investing 5% more while withdrawing 5% more from our freedom accounts until all current income came from our freedom accounts. I call this the "Independence Growing at 5% Per Year Plan." Table 4.1 shows the details of how this plan works, assuming we earn 10% per year on our investments.

I know some will argue that a 10%-per-year investment gain is too high of an assumption. However, I challenge my readers to find any twenty-year period in which the S&P 500 has not achieved that level of return or higher. Also, it's important to understand that the interest or investment gain will not be enough to support the withdrawal from the freedom account for several years. But remember that in every year we will be depositing 20% more of our income than we are withdrawing. This difference plus the investment gains will allow our freedom accounts to continue to grow until they will support all our withdrawals. Furthermore, it is important to understand that the freedom account will still work even with zero investment gains. If you need proof, visit www.poor-no-more.com and download the freedom account Excel spreadsheet and enter zero investment return to verify that the freedom account concept still works with zero return. We will address investments in chapters 15, 16, and 17.

In Table 4.1, we use a $100,000-per-year after-tax income as an example. There is nothing magical about this income level other than it makes it easy to convert the table's income assumptions to our personal income levels. For a take-home income of $25,000 per year, simply divide the numbers in the table by 4. For an income of $50,000 per year, divide by 2, and for $160,000 per year, multiply by 1.60. Or go to www.poor-no-more.com and download that freedom account Excel spreadsheet that will help you do the calculation for your individual situation in much greater detail than the tables in this book.

By examining Table 4.1, we see that by the end of year five we have a net investment contribution of 20% per year for five years, which totals 100% of our annual take-home income. However, due to the power of compounding returns, our freedom account balance has grown to 122% of a year's employment income.

At the end of year ten we have investment contributions totaling 200% of a year's employment income while our freedom account balance has grown to 318% of a year's income. And at the end of fifteen years we have invested 300% of a year's employment income while our freedom account balance has grown to 635% of a year's income. Now the freedom account balance grows very rapidly since we are withdrawing increasingly little compared to the portfolio's investment income.

The above example is just that - an example. Alternative formulas such as the one in Table 4.2 could be used. Table 4.2 uses a step-up method of 5% plus one more percent each year. I call this the "Independence Growing at 5%, 6%, 7%, 8%, 9% Per Year Plan." Although this plan allows us to live off our freedom account earlier, it does not make our freedom account balance grow more quickly, because on net we are still investing 20% per year. This is the difference between our contributions and our withdrawals from our freedom account. *See Table 4.2.*

To make our freedom accounts grow more quickly, we will need a higher level of net annual investment. Table 4.3 gives an example that starts with a 25% contribution to our freedom account and steps up 5% per year. This higher level of net contribution to our freedom accounts leads to much faster independence.

I know some people will say, "But the numbers in these tables don't account for inflation and taxes!" This is true, but these tables also don't account for incomes growing faster than the inflation rate and thus allowing the freedom account owner more funds to pay the taxes on the gains. Also, many of the freedom account's assets will be in retirement accounts that are taxed-deferred.

These critics miss the point. These plans intend to help us:

1) To save more.
2) To control our expenses.
3) To learn how to live off investment income.
4) To achieve financial independence early in our lives.
5) To encourage savings due to nearer-term benefits versus retirement.

But if you want to be a purist, please go to www.poor-no-more.com and download the freedom account Excel spreadsheet and enter any assumptions that you want. This spreadsheet will verify that the freedom account concept works in almost all circumstances.

Table 4.2
Freedom Account Dynamics
Independence Growing at 5%, 6%, 7%, 8%, 9%
with 20% Start

Year	After-Tax Income	Percent Contribution to Freedom Account	Cash Contribution to Freedom Account	10% Interest on Prior Year Ending Balance	Percent Withdrawal for Current Year Support	Cash Withdrawal for Current Year Support	Freedom Account Year Ending Balance
1	$100,000	20.0%	$20,000	$0	0.0%	$0	$20,000
2	$100,000	25.0%	$25,000	$2,000	5.0%	-$5,000	$42,000
3	$100,000	31.0%	$31,000	$4,200	11.0%	-$11,000	$66,200
4	$100,000	38.0%	$38,000	$6,620	18.0%	-$18,000	$92,820
5	$100,000	46.0%	$46,000	$9,282	26.0%	-$26,000	$122,102
6	$100,000	55.0%	$55,000	$12,210	35.0%	-$35,000	$154,312
7	$100,000	65.0%	$65,000	$15,431	45.0%	-$45,000	$189,743
8	$100,000	76.0%	$76,000	$18,974	56.0%	-$56,000	$228,718
9	$100,000	88.0%	$88,000	$22,872	68.0%	-$68,000	$271,590
10	$100,000	100.0%	$100,000	$27,159	80.0%	-$80,000	$318,748
11	$100,000	100.0%	$100,000	$31,875	80.0%	-$80,000	$370,623
12	$100,000	100.0%	$100,000	$37,062	80.0%	-$80,000	$427,686
13	$100,000	100.0%	$100,000	$42,769	80.0%	-$80,000	$490,454
14	$100,000	100.0%	$100,000	$49,045	80.0%	-$80,000	$559,500
15	$100,000	100.0%	$100,000	$55,950	80.0%	-$80,000	$635,450
16	$100,000	100.0%	$100,000	$63,545	80.0%	-$80,000	$718,995
17	$100,000	100.0%	$100,000	$71,899	80.0%	-$80,000	$810,894
18	$100,000	100.0%	$100,000	$81,089	80.0%	-$80,000	$911,983
19	$100,000	100.0%	$100,000	$91,198	80.0%	-$80,000	$1,023,182
20	$100,000	100.0%	$100,000	$102,318	80.0%	-$80,000	$1,145,500
21	$100,000	100.0%	$100,000	$114,550	80.0%	-$80,000	$1,280,050
22	$100,000	100.0%	$100,000	$128,005	80.0%	-$80,000	$1,428,055
23	$100,000	100.0%	$100,000	$142,805	80.0%	-$80,000	$1,590,860
24	$100,000	100.0%	$100,000	$159,086	80.0%	-$80,000	$1,769,947
25	$100,000	100.0%	$100,000	$176,995	80.0%	-$80,000	$1,966,941
26	$100,000	100.0%	$100,000	$196,694	80.0%	-$80,000	$2,183,635
27	$100,000	100.0%	$100,000	$218,364	80.0%	-$80,000	$2,421,999
28	$100,000	100.0%	$100,000	$242,200	80.0%	-$80,000	$2,684,199
29	$100,000	100.0%	$100,000	$268,420	80.0%	-$80,000	$2,972,619
30	$100,000	100.0%	$100,000	$297,262	80.0%	-$80,000	$3,289,880
31	$100,000	100.0%	$100,000	$328,988	80.0%	-$80,000	$3,638,868
32	$100,000	100.0%	$100,000	$363,887	80.0%	-$80,000	$4,022,755
33	$100,000	100.0%	$100,000	$402,276	80.0%	-$80,000	$4,445,031
34	$100,000	100.0%	$100,000	$444,503	80.0%	-$80,000	$4,909,534
35	$100,000	100.0%	$100,000	$490,953	80.0%	-$80,000	$5,420,487

Table 4.3
Freedom Account Dynamics
Independence Growing at 5% with 25% Start

Year	After-Tax Income	Percent Contribution to Freedom Account	Cash Contribution to Freedom Account	10% Interest on Prior Year Ending Balance	Percent Withdrawal for Current Year Support	Cash Withdrawal for Current Year Support	Freedom Account Year Ending Balance
1	$100,000	25.0%	$25,000	$0	0.0%	$0	$25,000
2	$100,000	30.0%	$30,000	$2,500	5.0%	-$5,000	$52,500
3	$100,000	35.0%	$35,000	$5,250	10.0%	-$10,000	$82,750
4	$100,000	40.0%	$40,000	$8,275	15.0%	-$15,000	$116,025
5	$100,000	45.0%	$45,000	$11,603	20.0%	-$20,000	$152,628
6	$100,000	50.0%	$50,000	$15,263	25.0%	-$25,000	$192,890
7	$100,000	55.0%	$55,000	$19,289	30.0%	-$30,000	$237,179
8	$100,000	60.0%	$60,000	$23,718	35.0%	-$35,000	$285,897
9	$100,000	65.0%	$65,000	$28,590	40.0%	-$40,000	$339,487
10	$100,000	70.0%	$70,000	$33,949	45.0%	-$45,000	$398,436
11	$100,000	75.0%	$75,000	$39,844	50.0%	-$50,000	$463,279
12	$100,000	80.0%	$80,000	$46,328	55.0%	-$55,000	$534,607
13	$100,000	85.0%	$85,000	$53,461	60.0%	-$60,000	$613,068
14	$100,000	90.0%	$90,000	$61,307	65.0%	-$65,000	$699,375
15	$100,000	95.0%	$95,000	$69,937	70.0%	-$70,000	$794,312
16	$100,000	100.0%	$100,000	$79,431	75.0%	-$75,000	$898,743
17	$100,000	100.0%	$105,000	$89,874	75.0%	-$75,000	$1,018,618
18	$100,000	100.0%	$100,000	$101,862	75.0%	-$75,000	$1,145,479
19	$100,000	100.0%	$100,000	$114,548	75.0%	-$75,000	$1,285,027
20	$100,000	100.0%	$100,000	$128,503	75.0%	-$75,000	$1,438,530
21	$100,000	100.0%	$100,000	$143,853	75.0%	-$75,000	$1,607,383
22	$100,000	100.0%	$100,000	$160,738	75.0%	-$75,000	$1,793,121
23	$100,000	100.0%	$100,000	$179,312	75.0%	-$75,000	$1,997,433
24	$100,000	100.0%	$100,000	$199,743	75.0%	-$75,000	$2,222,177
25	$100,000	100.0%	$100,000	$222,218	75.0%	-$75,000	$2,469,394
26	$100,000	100.0%	$100,000	$246,939	75.0%	-$75,000	$2,741,334
27	$100,000	100.0%	$100,000	$274,133	75.0%	-$75,000	$3,040,467
28	$100,000	100.0%	$100,000	$304,047	75.0%	-$75,000	$3,369,514
29	$100,000	100.0%	$100,000	$336,951	75.0%	-$75,000	$3,731,465
30	$100,000	100.0%	$100,000	$373,147	75.0%	-$75,000	$4,129,612
31	$100,000	100.0%	$100,000	$412,961	75.0%	-$75,000	$4,567,573
32	$100,000	100.0%	$100,000	$456,757	75.0%	-$75,000	$5,049,330
33	$100,000	100.0%	$100,000	$504,933	75.0%	-$75,000	$5,579,263
34	$100,000	100.0%	$100,000	$557,926	75.0%	-$75,000	$6,162,190
35	$100,000	100.0%	$100,000	$616,219	75.0%	-$75,000	$6,803,409

But don't go to a bank or brokerage firm and ask to open a freedom account. Unless this book becomes extremely popular, they will have no idea what type of account this is. A freedom account is my own concept that can be applied to traditional financial structures. Our freedom accounts could be composed of several types of accounts. We need to choose which types of accounts are appropriate for our situations. I suggest considering a combination of 401(k) accounts, SEP IRA accounts, Roth IRA accounts, Traditional IRA accounts, and standard brokerage accounts.

For people with a 401(k) program available, I suggest investing 15% per year into their 401(k), plus another 10% into a brokerage investment account. Although this totals 25% per year, it only costs 20% a year after taxes due to the tax deduction for the 401(k) contribution. The 401(k) matching plans that some employers provide could make our 15% 401(k) contribution even larger with the matching.

We need to be careful how we allocate among our account types. Avoid having too much money in illiquid retirement accounts. Remember, we need to take out regular withdrawals from our freedom account, and most retirement accounts have tax implications for early withdrawals. On the other hand, we want to maximize the amount of contribution to retirement accounts so that we can minimize taxes or investments, plus take advantage of tax deductions we get for making contributions. The people at www.poor-no-more.com can help you balance these issues and form the optimal structure. Download the freedom account Excel spreadsheet from www.poor-no-more.

com to work out how much to put in taxable accounts versus tax-deferred retirement accounts.

Chapter Takeaway

Freedom accounts work because the benefits we receive are in the very near term, not multiple decades away like the benefits from retirement accounts. Freedom accounts work because we feel, almost immediately, the growing ability to live off our investments. They work because they make us feel less dependent on our paychecks and contribute to our feeling of financial serenity.

The freedom account concept is superior to traditional retirement planning and retirement saving for the following reasons:

1) The benefits start almost immediately instead of decades in the future.
2) It is much easier to commit to increase saving when the benefits are nearer term.
3) The additional liquidity allows us to take more career risks resulting in higher pay.
4) Training ourselves to live off investment income early in life makes good sense.
5) Believing we can abruptly switch to comfortably living off investment income late in life is not reasonable, and is a major problem with traditional retirement planning.

The goal is to live off our investments and not off our paychecks. In time paychecks just become another instrument for increasing our investment pool. Establishing wealth can be defined as living off our investments instead of off our paychecks.

Chapter 5
Madison Avenue Versus Us

How can we possibly find extra money to put into a freedom account when we don't have enough money now to pay our bills? Why do we never seem to have enough money to pay our bills? Why don't we ever seem to have enough money to save? Why can't we get out of debt? We must answer these questions in order to have the money available to fund our freedom accounts. In fact, we must solve these problems in order to enjoy our lives.

There is a tug-of-war between corporations and consumers to gain control of our dollars and desires. With corporations no longer being content to sell us what we need, they have invested billions perfecting the science of mass media marketing designed to convince us that we need their products, useful or not. Honestly, who really needs a Chia Pet?

This has been an unfair tug-of-war. Corporations' enormous budgets can drown consumers with a flood of marketing. This marketing can create feelings of need and desire within consumers that do not naturally exist. Unfortunately, these false needs are unwillingly implanted into our belief systems without our knowledge and without regard to our true needs. Further, these false needs are implanted without regard to their affordability. Not to worry though, Madison Avenue is also happy to convince us that it is okay to buy on credit.

Corporations don't want us to think; they just want us to compulsively buy based on their marketing.

I believe that we simply do not need a third of what we buy and that artificial desires or needs for things have been created by mass marketing. I also believe that most consumers have surrendered or have lost control of their desires due to mass advertising. If we save the third of our money that we waste on these unnecessary purchases, we could easily fund our freedom accounts.

Consumers seem to no longer ask questions like: "Do I really need this?" or "Can I afford this?" They rarely properly examine the issue of affordability. They tend to erroneously look only at the monthly payment or availability of credit to determine if they can afford a purchase. "Well, the credit manager said I could afford it." Consumers lack the skills to determine what they can actually afford. Instead, they often buy because they think the product is cool or neat without regard to affordability. They seem to forget that everything they buy needlessly results in something else they can't buy, which they may really need.

Paramount to our financial success, we must recognize that Madison Avenue advertising executives have declared war on our good senses.

Madison Avenue's goal is nothing short of mind control. We have seen this plot before in movies in which an "evil scientist" tries to take over the world by controlling our minds. Watching these movies, we boo the evil scientist and praise the hero who foils his evil plans. In real life, there is no hero and we financially support the evil scientist by applying for credit to buy his unneeded products.

For example, we often buy products due to their perceived convenience or advantage. The comedian Ellen DeGeneres alluded to this in one of her routines, which went something like:

"I used to suck on breath mints. Now I use breath strips that dissolve in my mouth. When did I become too lazy to suck?"

Ellen's comedic observation reveals two issues. First, a desire has been created in her without her knowledge or consent. Second, the unwillingly implanted perceived convenience or advantage of the new product is questionable at best. The bad news is that we purchase most items in our lives without realizing that the desire for the product has been unwittingly injected into our psyches.

When did we lose the ability to distinguish between want and need? I personally believe many consumers no longer see any difference. So let me explain the important difference. A purchase made due to a want or a desire may give us a perceived pleasure. However, little if any real difference will result in our lives because of the purchase. In contrast, not having the resources to satisfy our basic needs can have a profound effect on our lives. The lack of a "want" will have little effect on our lives. However, the lack of a "need" could end our lives.

Our "needs" include purchases related to basic food, shelter, clothing, health, safety, transportation, socializing, and saving in our freedom accounts. However, don't fall into the trap that the desire for a $100 steak dinner has anything to do with the need for food.

Buying breath strips instead of breath mints is an example of surrendering to a "want," since either product would satisfy the social need for inoffensive breath. Buying that new pair of must-have shoes when we already have forty-seven pairs in our closet is another example of surrendering to a want. However, my wife takes exception to this last example.

I'm not saying we shouldn't buy things we want. The important issue here is for us to be aware of whether our purchases are "wants" or "needs" and therefore regain control of our expenditures. We must make sure our purchase decisions are our own and not decisions imposed on us by advertising executives. Often people can't buy what they truly need because they've spent too much money on items that are only "wants".

Do we wish to control what we buy, or should we allow strangers working on Madison Avenue to put their hands in our wallets?

We have to understand that there is a war for control of our minds. Corporations drive their incomes by controlling our minds and purchase decisions. Therefore, we mustn't fully trust our sense of need and must instead ask ourselves some questions to help us to determine if the need is real or if it has been implanted by Madison Avenue. When standing in a store about to make a purchase, here are some tips and questions you may want to consider:

1) Consider recently viewed advertisements on this product that could unduly affect your decision to buy. Don't let Madison Avenue win!

2) Do you hear a product jingle or celebrity endorsement ringing in your head as you are considering a purchase? Saint Patrick led the snakes out of Ireland with a flute. Is this happening to you?

3) Are you buying a new product that replaces an existing product? Does the old product no longer meet the need? Can the old product be used longer?

4) Is there a more practical substitute product? More practical could be defined as servicing the need at a lower cost, better servicing the need, or servicing additional needs as well.

5) What are you willing to give up in order to purchase the item you are considering? It is a financial fact of life that every product you buy results in something else you can't buy.

6) Is this purchase within your budget? If not, don't even consider the purchase. The problem with this simple truth is that most people don't have a budget. Budgeting will be discussed more in chapter 7.

7) The most basic and important issue is to distinguish between wants and needs. The ability to distinguish is critical and often determines financial success or failure. I have a friend driving around in his brand-new Corvette. He keeps getting his utilities cut off because he is short of cash. It's fine to buy wanted items we don't really need. However, these purchases should come after our needs are covered, including funding our financial freedom accounts.

If we follow these rules, more items will be left on the shelves during our next store visit. Now think about adding the money we just saved to our freedom accounts.

The evilest weapon that Madison Avenue advertising executives deploy against us is advertising to our children.

Madison Avenue knows that it is easier and more effective to brainwash our children to crave advertised products than to brainwash us. I've often seen children whining for items in stores and then seen the parents acquiescing, buying the items in order to stop the whining. This is questionable parenting.

Instead, parents need to keep control and use the same purchase rationale for their children as they do for themselves. Furthermore, they must remember that every time they succumb to a child's whining, all they have done is train the child to whine again. The short-term cessation of the whining will be followed by more whining now that the child knows that whining works. If we allow Madison Avenue to control our kids, we are allowing them to control us through our kids. We must regain control.

If Madison Avenue advertising is convincing us to buy things we don't need, why don't we turn off the advertising? Good question. How do we turn off the advertising?

Instead of watching broadcast TV, which is one-third advertising, why not just rent DVDs? Consider viewing premium channels without advertising. Or maybe learn something by watching PBS. Many popular broadcast TV shows are available on DVD within a year of their original broadcast. Buy or rent and then view the DVDs without being subjected to advertising. Or buy a DVR system that can remove the advertising.

While in the car, listen to CDs or an iPod instead of broadcast radio. Consider buying a satellite radio system. Or listen to public radio. Or if all else fails, listen to an audio book about personal finance. My point is that *we* control the off switch. Take control!

Chapter Takeaway

Corporations don't want us to think. They want us to buy compulsively.

We must realize a war is being waged to control our minds and purchase decisions.

We must win this war and take back control of our lives. Coming to this realization and learning to master the seven tips shown above will reduce most consumers' wasteful expenditures significantly without any reduction of lifestyle. We must regain control of our purchasing decisions. Small savings from here and there can add up to a lot. Often, the savings from the above concepts alone result in enough free cash to fund many consumers' financial freedom accounts.

Chapter 6
Our "NEEDS" Versus Our "WANTS"

We have been brainwashed by advertising all of our lives. Due to these influences, we buy things we don't need because unnatural desires have been placed in our psyches by repetitious marketing. We waste money buying items we don't need or use. We must realize that we have lost control and that it will be a struggle to regain control. We need to recapture the money wasted on things we don't need and redirect those funds to our freedom accounts.

First, we must realize that we cannot trust our instincts and beliefs because they have been corrupted by years of advertising. Second, we must develop systematic or formulaic methods of determining our needs and differentiating them from our wants. These methods must be isolated from our instincts and beliefs, which have been corrupted by advertising. Third, when making purchase decisions, we should determine if the product satisfies a need or simply a want. We must then provide for all our needs before we consider any wants.

Let's start by defining these two categories.

> NEED: A product whose absence will have a profound effect on our lives.

> WANT: A product that may give a perceived pleasure.

It is important to separate the two categories so that we can provide for all our needs before we purchase "nice to have" wants. As simple as this concept is, many consumers only think "I want, I want, I want." I believe that this impulse is one of the causes behind the growing numbers of bankrupt families.

The simple definition above helps to separate our needs from our wants. However, further evaluation is required here. It is not sufficient that a product being considered for purchase meets the definition of being a need. We should also verify its status as a need by determining if it fits into one of the eight predefined categories below.

Traditionally, needs have been defined as food, shelter, and clothing. However, I have expanded this basic list of three to eight by including health care, safety, transportation, socializing, and our financial freedom account. Now let's examine each of these categories.

1) BASIC FOOD. This category includes only the food we purchase to prepare and eat at home or carry to work as our lunches. Home-prepared food is the most economical and thus the only food that meets the basic need. This category excludes restaurants and fast food, which instead fall under the want category.

2) BASIC SHELTER. This category includes the rent or mortgage (including equity lines of credit) necessary to provide a reasonably-sized, safe, and well-located residence. Basic shelter includes home insurance,

property taxes, and the cost of required utilities such as water, electricity, sanitation, gas, and heating oil. Note: This category does not include cable or satellite television, high-speed Internet services, or maid services; these fall under the want category.

3) BASIC CLOTHING. This category is harder to define because our basic requirements vary with career choices and social situations. As a guideline, a professional, wearing suits every day, should cap basic annual expenditures to under 4% of gross income. Others should cap annual expenditures to under 2%. This category should include expenses related to dry cleaning and laundry. Additional expenditures on clothing fall under the want category.

4) BASIC HEALTH CARE. This category includes health insurance, doctor and dentist visits, glasses and contacts, prescriptions, co-pays, over-the-counter drugs, and toiletries. Toiletries include toothpaste, mouthwash, razor blades, deodorant, soap, and similar items. This category does not include breast augmentations, hair implants, Botox injections, and plastic surgeries.

5) BASIC SAFETY. This category includes reasonable expenditures required to remove unsafe hazards from our lives and/or properties. It could include alarm systems, fire extinguishers, smoke detectors, outside lighting systems, walkway lighting, and motion detection systems. New locks, better windows, better doors, and improved balcony or stair railings could be included

in this category. It could also include expenditures due to moving from an unsafe employer, neighborhood, marriage, or relationship. Often expenditures in this category reduce expenses due to theft and injuries. This category does not include lethal weapons of any kind.

6) **BASIC TRANSPORTATION.** This category includes the minimum amount required for a daily employment commute, plus other social and family mobility needs. This does not always mean a private car. This category could include the cost of a car, car repair, car insurance, gasoline, bus fare, train fare, parking, and car registration. Many people say that they greatly prefer driving their cars versus taking public transportation. Yet many of these same people have never tried public transportation. Let me suggest using public transportation for one week and comparing the savings before rejecting it.

7) **BASIC SOCIALIZING.** This category includes the basic socializing expenses required to be happy with our lives and keep us from going nuts. Going out with friends, having dinner with friends, and participating in activities to meet new friends are all part of this expense category. To call this category a need is a gray area. The key is to control this expense. This category will vary wildly from person to person but should not exceed 5% of our income. Additional expenditures on socializing fall under the want category.

8) **FUND OUR FREEDOM ACCOUNTS.** Expenses in this category have already been defined in chapter 4 and should equal at least 20% of our gross income.

Now that we have defined our needs, it's very easy to define our wants. Our wants are everything that lies outside our needs. If the product does not fit into the basic definition of a need or does not fall within one of these expanded categories, it is merely a want and not a need.

The goal is to comfortably fulfill all our needs and find a way to get resources for many of our wants.

Chapter Takeaway

We should realize that we have lost control of our desires. We must use systematic and formulaic methods of determining our needs and differentiating them from our wants. These methods must be isolated from our instincts and beliefs, which have been corrupted by advertising. This chapter provides two tools (or screens) to help us determine if a product is actually needed or merely wanted.

The first screen is a simple definition we should apply to all our purchases. When considering any product purchase, we should ask ourselves if the product's absence would have a profound effect on our lives. If our answer is no, then this product is simply a want whose purchase should be considered only after all our needs are met.

If the product passes our first screen, then we must determine if the product fits within one of our eight basic need categories.

Only if the product passes both screens should we consider the product a needed item. Wanted items require more evaluation and should be purchased only after examining budget concerns.

We must find a way to adjust our lives so that we address all of our needs without going into debt and without struggling to make ends meet.

This can be done by properly and creatively going through the budgeting process and finding ways to live well "on-the-cheap." The next two chapters discuss how to do this while maximizing the pleasures of life.

We can improve our lifestyles if we eliminate the wasteful spending in our lives.

Chapter 7
Planning and Budgeting

Many people avoid budgeting because they fear the results will be bad news that will force them to eliminate activities they enjoy. However, the budgeting process should be viewed as an eye-opener and a tool to regain control of our lives. Often people incorrectly view a personal budget as some outside force restricting and controlling them. Remember, we are the masters of our personal budgets. Our budgets do not control us. A budget is just a tool to give us a clearer understanding of our personal finances.

We must view the financial part of our lives as a business, and as businesspeople, we must use basic management skills.

Business Management 101 states, "We can't improve it until we measure it."

Similarly, we cannot improve our personal finances until we measure them. The way we can begin to measure our personal finances is by completing a budget. A budget is simply an organized list of all our expenses. This list doesn't control us; it's just a tool to help us understand where we are. Therefore, we should begin with an honest list of how we currently spend our money so that we can understand our spending patterns.

We need to get our heads out of the sand, overcome our fears of what a budget may reveal, quit procrastinating, and complete our personal budgets before we can advance financially.

We must see where we are before we can plan where we are going.

A budget can illuminate some unnecessary expenses while hopefully showing us a path toward affording some extra luxuries. Budgeting is the first step on the path to financial freedom.

Completing a budget is not a one-time event. Instead, it is a multi-pass process we refine and perform regularly as we make improvements. We can expect our first pass to be depressing due to chilling revelations it might reveal about our spending patterns. Don't worry though! A budget is just a tool to help us regain control of our lives. As we regain control, we will feel better and more financially secure.

If we spend forty hours a week earning our income, isn't it prudent to spend thirty minutes a month planning how we spend it?

The budgeting process should begin at the basic needs level. Once we provide for our basic needs, then we can proceed with a budget that will include most of our wants.

Let's begin with the basic needs budget I have included below. Fill this out in a format that is easy to change, using a pencil or an Excel spreadsheet. A budget spreadsheet can be downloaded from www.poor-no-more.com. We will need to estimate many items, so try to be as accurate and as honest as possible. Looking at prior credit card bills and checking accounts may be helpful with making these estimates.

Note that this is a monthly budget. Therefore, expenses that occur on a weekly basis should be multiplied by 4.3 and converted to monthly expenses. Other less frequent expenses, such as doctor visits, should be added up on an annual basis and then divided by 12 for conversion to monthly expenses.

BASIC NEEDS BUDGET

1) BASIC FOOD

    Groceries   _____

2) BASIC SHELTER

    Rent   _____
    Renter's insurance   _____
    Or
    1st Mortgage   _____
    2nd Mortgage   _____
    *PMI (mortgage insurance)   _____
    Homeowner's association   _____
    Homeowner's insurance   _____
    Property taxes   _____
    Water utility   _____
    Electric utility   _____
    Natural gas utility   _____

Heating oil _____
Basic Internet service _____

3) BASIC CLOTHING

Dry cleaning _____
Laundry cost _____
Cost of New Clothes _____

4) BASIC HEALTHCARE

Health insurance _____
Doctor visits _____
Dentist visits _____
Corrective eyewear _____
Prescription drugs _____
Over-the-counter drugs _____
Birth control _____
Diapers _____
Children daycare _____
Toiletries _____
Haircuts _____

5) BASIC SAFETY

Alarm systems _____
Basic home phone service _____
Basic cell phone service _____
Other service/systems _____
Other repairs _____

6) BASIC TRANSPORTATION

Bus tickets or monthly pass _____
Train tickets or monthly pass _____
*Auto lease payment _____
*Auto loan payments _____
Auto repair budget _____
Auto maintenance -oil change _____
Auto title/license fees _____
Auto insurance _____
Auto gasoline _____
Parking lot fees _____
Toll road/bridge _____

7) BASIC SOCIALIZING (Category should be less than 5% of monthly income)

Coffee/drinks with friends _____
Lunch with friends/coworkers _____
Dinners with friends _____
Dating _____
Hobby _____
Other #1 _____
Other #2 _____

8) FUND FREEDOM ACCOUNT

Monthly income _____ × 0.2 = _____
* Budget items that should be avoided.

Debt hasn't been included in our basic budget because we should not have debt. Debt is the terrible legacy we have left ourselves due to prior excesses. Debt must be eliminated; chapter 9 will deal with this subject. If you have debt, it must be fully paid off before you can start to fund the freedom account. For the budgeting process, temporarily list all the debt payments instead of freedom account payments. Don't get trapped into believing that debt is a normal part of life!

I have included asterisks by budget items I believe should be avoided. However, I have included them in the basic budget because so many consumers have these expenses. This includes car loans or car lease payments that I will explain how to eliminate in chapters 10 and 11. This also includes PMI (Private Mortgage Insurance), which we will discuss in chapter 14.

Expenses should be added up and compared with after-tax income. If our budgeted basic needs expenses exceed our take-home income, we have a problem. However, we are not alone. Many people find themselves in similar straits. At least we now recognize the problem and are taking actions to improve the situation.

If the shortfall is small, congratulations. Simple lifestyle adjustments may be all that is needed. Following the purchase decision tips from chapters 5 and 6 could really help. Expense reductions in all categories are important because small savings add up. Chapter 8 will cover many other ways to save while simultaneously improving our lifestyles.

A larger shortfall will probably require adjustments in the transportation and shelter categories. Restructuring these categories can dramatically affect our expenses. Chapters 10, 11, and 14 address these categories. By reviewing these chapters, we may find ways to afford more of the pleasures of life.

Remember that budgeting is a multi-pass process that we refine and revise as we reduce our expenses. We should use the budgeting tool above coupled with the saving suggestions from this book to determine what is obtainable. The ultimate goal is a budget that allows us to have what we need first and then what we want.

This process does not happen overnight. It may take months to reduce our expenses to fit our income levels. Once our basic expenses are within our income levels, we can look at the next expense, i.e., debt.

Once we have met our basic needs and have paid off all debt, we can start adding extra wanted items back to our budgets. The following wants budget lists some extras we may want to add.

WANTS BUDGET

Cable/satellite TV	_____
DVD rental service	_____
DSL Internet service	_____
CDs and music downloads	_____
Dining out	_____
Maid services	_____
Gardener services	_____
Off-site storage facility	_____
New household electronics	_____
Additional clothing expenses	_____

Health/exercise clubs	_____
Social clubs	_____
Travel/vacation expenses	_____
More toys for children	_____
Gifts	_____
Children's private lessons	_____
Children's private schools	_____
Children's summer camps	_____
Sporting events	_____
Movies	_____
Concerts/plays	_____
Hobbies	_____
Golf expenses	_____
Jewelry	_____
Boating expenses	_____
RV expenses	_____
Omnibus vice account	_____
Other	_____

What is the omnibus vice account? Let's be honest, we all spend money on personal vices, gambling, cigars, shoes, sweets, or whatever our particular fancy might be. We should include these expenditures in our budget planning and thus gain more control over this type of expense.

What should we spend on each category? What should our budget look like on a percentage basis? Well, this depends a lot on our personal situations. However, I've provided a guideline below.

Suggested Breakdown of Personal Budgets

	Families	Singles
Food (groceries)	12%	11%
Shelter (housing & utilities)	37%	33%
Clothing (purchase & cleaning)	4%	4%
Health care (gym, doctor, insurance)	6%	6%
Safety	3%	3%
Transportation (purchase & operating)	13%	15%
Socializing (entertainment & dining)	5%	8%
Freedom account (saving & investment)	20%	20%
TOTAL =	100%	100%

Chapter Takeaway

Often people incorrectly view personal budgets as restricting and controlling. They avoid budgeting because they fear the results will be bad news and force them to eliminate fun activities. However, we absolutely cannot improve our finances until we understand and measure them. A budget is just a tool to give us a clearer understanding of our finances. We must complete a personal budget for ourselves regularly in order to track our progress toward financial freedom and success in obtaining everything we want.

POOR NO MORE

Chapter 8
Living Well on Less

Differentiating between what is needed and what is wanted is only part of the solution to controlling our expenses. We should strive to purchase what we need at affordable prices. The savings we find can then become contributions to our freedom accounts.

Buying items at more affordable prices should be viewed as a challenge or even a game. We should adopt the attitude that it is fun to buy quality items on the cheap. Viewing this as a sport would be a helpful concept. There are several categories in which we can stretch our money without limiting our lifestyles. These include:

1) Energy and utility cost reductions
2) Gasoline and transportation cost reductions
3) Interest cost reductions
4) Coupons and rebates
5) Internet transactions
6) Price guaranties
7) Purchase timing
8) Insurance costs
9) Other services' costs
10) Travel and vacation costs

Energy and Utility Cost Reductions
With today's rising energy costs, utilities are becoming an increasing share of our household expenses. However, there are many ways to save money on these necessary utilities. Plus, saving energy is the environmentally friendly, "green" thing to do.

Many people think the wattage rating on light bulbs is a measure of brightness. This is not true. The lumen rating is the true measurement of brightness. The wattage rating is actually an indication of the power consumed. Thus, a 40-watt light bulb uses $2/3$ of the power of a 60-watt light bulb. Replacing 60-watt bulbs with 40-watt bulbs reduces lighting costs by 33%. Using higher-wattage bulbs wastes energy and money.

If a light fixture has multiple bulbs, the light required from each bulb is less, so consider using lower-wattage bulbs, such as 15- or 25-watt bulbs. People seem to automatically buy 60-watt bulbs. This is wasteful. Also note that lower-wattage bulbs last longer, which saves replacement costs.

Using high-wattage bulbs wastes energy in another way. Wattage used equates to heat generated. During air-conditioning months, this extra wasteful heat must be overcome by running the air conditioner longer. We should review our light bulbs and reduce wattage where possible.

The lighting type we choose can dramatically affect our electric bills. The recent trend of using halogen lighting is uneconomical. Halogen lighting tends to have high wattage ratings and is therefore wasteful. Most of the power goes to generate heat rather than light. Let's get rid of those wasteful 300- and 500-watt halogen torch lamps.

The recent trend of using 12-volt lighting systems is also wasteful. Most 12-volt systems require transformers, which are inefficient and waste power. Let's avoid these systems.

Significant energy saving can also be accomplished by switching to fluorescent lights. I'm not suggesting that we put four-foot-long fluorescent lighting tubes in our ceilings. I'm talking about replacing ordinary 60- to 100-watt incandescent lamp-style bulbs with compact fluorescent bulbs. These bulbs have the same profile (size and shape) as an ordinary 60-watt screw-in lamp-style bulb and screw in to an ordinary lamp-style base. Major home improvement stores sell a six-pack of such bulbs for $9.99, and much lower prices are available online. These bulbs only consume 14 watts while producing as much light as a 60-watt traditional bulb. (Remember that the wattage rating is not a measure of light generated.) These compact fluorescent bulbs now come in different light color grades that allow us to select which color works best in our homes and with our eyes.

Switching to compact fluorescent bulbs is the right thing to do both for our wallets and for the environment. It's past time to stop the needless waste of energy and the unnecessary addition of greenhouse gases to our environment. At the time of this writing, seven states were considering legislation making the sale of traditional incandescent light bulbs illegal. Let's get ahead of the law change; do the right thing and replace incandescent bulbs.

According to Earth Day Network, "If every U.S. household replaced its light bulbs with energy-efficient compact fluorescent bulbs, the cumulative effect would lower our annual carbon dioxide emissions by 125 billion pounds."

What kind of savings can we expect? Let's assume we replace twenty ordinary 60-watt bulbs with 14-watt fluorescent bulbs. We would save 46 watts per bulb for a total of 920 watts. If these were used six hours a day, we would save about 5.5 kilowatt-hours per day, or about 2,000 kilowatt-hours per year. This equates to about $200 of annual savings. This is a significant saving considering that the twenty fluorescent bulbs only cost $40. The reduced heat production from the lower-wattage fluorescent bulbs would also reduce air-conditioning expenses, and the longer life of the compact fluorescent bulbs would also save us money.

Don't wait for your old light bulbs to burn out before going to fluorescents bulbs. It pays to make the switch ASAP.

I need to warn the reader that most fluorescent bulbs *do not work with dimmers.* I'm not talking about the three-level switches that some lamps have, but rather the gradual dimmers used in many wall light switches. Don't use normal florescent bulbs in these circuits, or replace the dimmer switch with a regular switch first. Recently, special dimmable fluorescent compact light bulbs have become available; these bulbs tend to be more readily available online than in hardware stores. Just go to www.eBay.com and search for "dimmable fluorescent."

Certain electronic light switches (some timer switches and remote-controllable switches) do not work well with regular compact fluorescent bulbs and result in a flickering of the fluorescent bulb. If this occurs, try a dimmable compact fluorescent bulb and the problem is often resolved.

LED light bulbs offer even higher savings. These 110-volt LED arrays only use 2 to 5 watts for the same amount of light as a 60-watt conventional bulb. They are generally available on the Internet. However, their light quality is different, so I suggest trying one before buying many. They are best suited to outside lighting.

To make the evaluation of savings easier, I would like to introduce the concept of a payback period. When considering a money saving project, since we are spending money, we should examine how long it takes to recover our expense. Generally, projects with shorter payback periods are more practical. In the previous fluorescent lighting example, $40 in new bulbs saves about $200 per year. Thus, the savings of $16 per month ($200/12) pays back the $40 investment in less than three months. This is an extremely short payback period and thus justifies paying for the new compact fluorescent light bulbs.

Before we spend money to save money, consider the payback period. A shorter payback period indicates a more practical project. We may wish to rank our projects in order of payback period to determine which we should do first. Savings on shorter payback projects could provide the funds for the longer payback projects. As an example, savings from compact fluorescent bulbs and a setback thermostat could allow us to afford a tank-less water heater. Savings from the new water heater could allow us to fund higher-efficiency windows.

Continuously maintaining a tank of hot water wastes energy. Consider replacing the water heater with a tank-less water heater. These heaters only heat water as needed. The payback for this project is often only nine to eighteen months, and these smaller heaters also result in additional storage space.

Replacing or adding weather stripping around doors and windows can also improve heating and cooling costs. Automatic setback thermostats can reduce these costs as well. These items have payback periods shorter than three months. The payback period is even shorter if self-installed.

Recently, I added solar reflective window film to ten south-facing windows in my home. A contractor charged me $269 to complete this task. I recorded a $150-a-month savings on my air-conditioning bill, making for less than a two-month payback. I don't recommend self-installation. The risks of bubbles and streaks from do-it-yourself kits are too high. Plus, selecting the incorrect film can cause some double pane windows to crack. Use an expert installer, but get several quotes first.

Consider replacing older single pane windows with new and efficient, vinyl double-pane windows. If we select the right contractor and windows, the payback for this kind of project is typically between twelve and twenty-four months. New windows will also insulate the home from outside road noise and add value to the property.

Adding attic insulation may have a short enough payback period to be justified. Installing a new high SER rated (higher efficiency) heating and cooling system may also be justified due to its increased efficiency.

The federal government has often offered tax credits to homeowners who install various energy saving products. However, these laws change a great deal from year to year. I recommend going to www.energystar.gov and then clicking on "tax credits" to get more information.

Often, the local utility encourages people to make these changes by rebating the cost of some of the above items. Check with the utility company.

Watering the lawn in the rain? A newer automatic lawn-watering controller that has rain sensors preventing this waste can be purchased for under $20. Also note that watering during the heat of the day is wasteful. Set the automatic controller to water at night.

I suggest reading the book *The Home Energy Diet* to learn more about this area. I further suggest using a web-based do-it-yourself energy audit tool to evaluate what home energy-saving techniques are appropriate. Check out www.hes.lbl.gov. Also check out the useful links tab at www.eere.energy.gov.

Whenever hiring a contractor to install anything, get several quotes, no fewer than three. Often, smaller contractors have lower overhead and can offer lower quotes. Only accept written fixed price quotes, not hourly rates with estimates from a previously unknown contractor. However, hourly rates may be cheaper if the contractor is known and trusted. Verify through the Internet that contractors are properly licensed and insured before awarding a job.

Gasoline and Transportation Cost Reductions

Chapters 10 and 11 will discuss how to save money purchasing our cars. This chapter addresses how to save money driving the cars we already own. As an example, we waste money because we misunderstand the differences between gasoline grades.

Most gasoline stations sell three grades of gasoline. What are the differences between the three grades? Why do people pay considerably more for the higher grade? Forgetting about the truth for a moment, I wanted to learn what the public believed the differences are. So I asked ten well-educated and otherwise intelligent people. Five of these people stated that the difference was the quality of the gas - the higher the grade; the better it is for your car. Two people believed the higher grades provide higher gas mileage. Two believed the higher grades provide better speed and acceleration performance. One person believed the higher grades prevent engine knocking.

I then asked five experienced auto mechanics and got similar results although more absolute in their opinions. Three said higher grades reflect the gasoline's quality, and two said higher grades prevent engine knocking and pinging. With the massive amount of misinformation out there, it is not surprising that all fifteen people got the answer wrong.

Here is the truth. The octane rating of gasoline reflects the speed at which a flame propagates as the gas burns. The higher the octane rating is, the slower the speed of the flame. Thus, higher-grade gasoline burns slower. Does this mean that slower-burning gas is higher-quality gasoline? The answer is no.

Gasoline's octane rating is a design parameter. The engine designer must shape the combustion chamber to properly optimize for the speed of the flame propagation. Using a grade of gasoline above or below the engine designer's assumptions will result in sub-optimum performance and lower fuel economy. Using a higher-grade gasoline than an engine is designed for will actually reduce, rather than improve, the performance. Most American-made cars are designed for regular gas. The original designer states which gas grade is required in the owner's manual. A mechanic does not have the engineering education to determine what fuel grade should be used. Only the gas grade that the owner's manual suggests should be used.

Many drivers and mechanics incorrectly state that higher-grade gasoline will prevent engine knocking or pinging. However, knocking and pinging is caused by pre-ignition of the gas. This is due to carbon buildup, aged spark plugs, or bad ignition timing. The fix to the above is not gasoline. The fix is a tune-up or possibly using a gas treatment additive to clean the carbon out of the engine. A slower-burning, higher-octane gas may reduce the effect of pre-ignition; however, it is not a fix. It is just a bandaid.

The American love affair with cars is the greatest budget-busting item families need to address. Chapters 10 and 11 are dedicated to this issue. However, there is a more basic problem regarding transportation costs. Most Americans drive their cars too much. This is because Americans tend to avoid public transportation like the plague. Why is this? Again, mass marketing has taken control of our minds and placed a stigma on public transportation while promoting private cars instead.

I have a friend - let's call him Dick - who was suffering financially due to a career choice that provided little income and a long commute. He was filling his gas tank three times a week plus paying $140 a month to park at his job. The wear and tear on his older car was generating repair bills. Breakdowns were also affecting his ability to reliably arrive at work.

After several people urged him, he finally tried mass transit. His mass transit commute wasn't easy. He had to drive to the train station, take a train downtown, take the subway to get close, and finally take a bus for the last few miles. His morning commute increased from about one hour to one and a half hours. His afternoon commute remained about the same because mass transit avoids traffic.

Was it worth moving to mass transit? Well, the transit pass was only $59 per month, and he saved over $500 a month in gasoline and parking costs. His car repair bills dropped to nothing. His monetary savings amounted to 30% of his total paycheck. He was able to sleep and read on mass transit and thus relax from the stress of driving.

If mass transit worked for the complicated commute that Dick had, could it work for you? What will the extra saving mean to your budget? What extra "wants" could you buy with the savings?

Interest Cost Reductions
Since most Americans have debt, most Americans pay interest. Improving your credit score can dramatically lower your interest costs. However, most Americans don't know or monitor their credit scores. Many Americans who think they have good credit simply don't. Let's get our heads out of the sand and learn how to manage our credit scores. Chapter 13 addresses this issue.

Home mortgage refinancing often saves money. Don't move too hastily on this. See chapter 14 for more details about how to save on mortgages.

Coupons and Rebates
Using grocery coupons can significantly reduce grocery costs. Often grocery stores will double the value of coupons, thus doubling our savings. Double coupons coupled with a grocery store sale can result in a virtually free purchase.

How do we find coupons? We no longer need to search our newspapers. There are many Web sites that provide free printable coupons. Below are just a few grocery-related coupon sites:

www.GroceryGame.com
www.Coupons.com
www.Albertsons.com
www.ConsumerIncentiveZone.com
www.CoolSavings.com
www.Eversave.com

Grocery coupons aren't the only things we find online. A wealth of discount coupons can be found on the Internet. Some of these coupons are used with online retailers, and many others were designed to be printed out and taken to the local store.

Buying anything without checking if a coupon is available is like throwing money away.

Listed below are just a few of the websites that offer coupons, discounts, and other valuable information for non-grocery retailers.

General Merchandise Coupons
www.TheCouponSpot.com
www.FastCouponCode.com
www.CouponCraze.com
www.wow-coupons.com
www.HotCoupons.com
www.eCoupons.com
www.UltimateCoupons.com
www.BradsDeals.com
www.PriceProtector.com
www.Savings-Center.com

Technology, Electronics, Computers, and Stuff
www.Slickdeals.net
www.Shopica.com
www.Javadeals.com
www.DealUnion.com
www.frys.com

Gift Programs
(These programs often require a subscription or other action.)

www.FreebieFanatic.com
www.IncentiveLeader.com
www.AllFreeGifts.net

Travel Related
www.site59.com
www.Motel-Coupons.com

More coupon sites can be found at www.poor-no-more.com.

Internet Transactions

Also realize that many items can be purchased on the Internet at a lower price. When seeing a desirable product, stop, go home, and find out how it is priced on the Internet. Often, significant savings can be found. More importantly, the extra time to think about the purchase could prevent us from making an unneeded spontaneous transaction. Impulse buying is a killer for the budget.

I like a particular type of razor blade that is a little costly. A four-pack of razors costs $11.99 at the grocery store and $9.99 at the discount store. However, on the Internet I can purchase a sixteen-pack of the same razors for $15.99. That's $1.00 a blade on the Internet versus $2.50 a blade at the discount store. This is typical of Internet savings.

Vitamins, over-the-counter drugs, prescription drugs, toiletries, music, DVDs, books, printer cartridges, and electronics are just a few examples of items commonly less expensive on the Internet. Generally, the best Internet savings can be obtained on smaller, lighter-weight items that are normally priced between $10 and $100. Very low-price or hard-to-ship items are best bought in brick-and-mortar stores rather than online stores.

Items purchased on the Internet have the extra expense of shipping. However, saving on the sales tax may offset this expense. Some in-state vendors will charge sales tax while most out-of-state vendors won't. Don't just search the price of the item, but also review its shipping costs as these may vary greatly among vendors.

Concerned about giving credit card info online? Get over it! Internet fraud comes primarily from firms that seek us out and not the other way around. Internet transactions with reputable sites are highly secure. However, to increase our protection, I recommend using a credit card with only a $300 to $500 limit for all Internet transactions. The lower limit reduces our exposure to fraud on the Internet.

Price Guarantees
There are many retail stores that offer price guarantees or price protection polices. We've all heard their claims about matching the price if we can find a better-advertised price. These policies state that if they or a competitor offer a better price within a certain time frame, they will refund the difference. The problem with these plans is that we have to watch the prices to be able to get these refunds. Who has time for this?

Once again the Internet provides a solution. The website www.PriceProtectr.com allows us to enter a product's bar code number, price that we paid, date that we purchased it, and store that we purchased the item from, and the site will watch for various prices that could trigger a price guaranty or price protector. By the way, I did not misspell "PriceProtectr" - "PriceProtector" is an unrelated coupon site.

Purchase Timing

Allowing for flexible purchase timing can also bring significant savings. Let me give an example. Many people's refrigerators contain a light bulb and not much more. Their owners go out each day and buy what they need for that day alone. This is a forced purchase, which is never a wise or practical way to buy.

Many groceries do not spoil quickly and thus can be purchased in volume and stored until needed. We should buy these items in larger quantities when they are on sale. Promotional discounts can often be as high as 40% and thus can result in significant savings. This deal can be sweetened even more if we use double coupons.

Almost everything in a grocery store will be offered at a sale discount at some time during the month. Why not allow ourselves the flexibility, through personal stockpiling, to wait for the sales? It may take a little extra cash in the beginning to build up our stockpiles; however, flexibility in our purchase timing offers large savings.

Often, people buy the smallest quantity package in an attempt to reduce current expenses. This is short-sighted and wrong thinking. We should buy in volume when that larger quantity offers savings. Notice that large volume does not always mean lower per unit pricing. Many stores offer unit pricing that can help in making volume purchase decisions. There are also large discount stores that specialize in volume pricing. Take advantage of them when they offer savings.

Purchase timing also applies to the fashion industry. Most items that come to a retail store will be on sale within six weeks. Timing our purchases helps to find lower prices. Roofers' quotes are generally lower during the dry season. Lawn furniture and outdoor barbeques are often much cheaper in September than in May. Christmas decorations are often used year after year and are much less expensive in January. Car deals are often better on the last day of the month. Get the idea? The point is to think about the timing before buying.

Insurance Costs
It's amazing how people buy car insurance from their car dealers and never shop for better rates.

Auto and home insurance is another area in which many of us can save money. Prices vary a great deal in this industry, so I suggest getting at least three quotes each year. Make sure one or two of the quotes are from a mutual insurance company. These are policyholder-owned companies that don't have a profit motive and therefore often have better rates and coverage. AMICA and USAA are good examples.

Also examine insurance deductible options. I have seen auto insurance quotes for which a $500 deductible cost $250 more per year than a $1,000 deductible. In this case, the extra $500 of insurance coverage cost $250 per year. How often do we have accidents? Unless we wreck our cars more than once in two years, it is less expensive to have the $1,000 deductible. Increasing policy deductibles should be considered.

How we title our car insurance can also result in significant savings. If both husband and wife have good driving records but have separate car insurance companies, substantial savings can be obtained by combining the separate policies into one policy. Often 35% savings are possible. Additional savings can be found if both the auto and homeowner policies are issued by the same company.

However, the reverse may be true if one spouse has a bad or new driving record. In this case, separate car insurance policies may provide the lowest total cost. If both policies allow the other spouse to drive, it may be best to insure the lower-value car with the spouse who has the bad or new driving record.

We should also shop our life insurance every couple of years. As life expectancies grow, rates decline. Often a lower rate can be found on a newer policy.

Other Services' Costs

Frequently examine Internet, phone, and cell phone service contracts to see if better offerings are available. Verify the termination fee on old contracts before making any changes.

Verify and compare the cost of cable TV versus satellite services. Review premium channels. Relying on a service like Netflix could be cheaper than subscribing to premium channels.

Off-site storage is expensive and often unnecessary. People store things they just end up throwing away after paying storage space rental for a few years. Try to reduce this expense. If you have not used an item in a year, it may be time to let go. Lighten the load! Gifts to friends, eBay sales, garage sales, and tax-deductible donations may be the right answer for these items.

Travel and Vacation Costs

Vacation and travel costs are another area in which significant savings can be made. For instance, time-share exchange companies often have excess capacity in their systems for sale even to people who don't own a time-share. Sometimes a week-long time-share condo rental is cheaper than a two-night stay in a hotel.

Speaking of time-shares, never buy one at retail prices. I suggest buying from individuals who are seeking to sell theirs. We can find such deals on the Internet. I purchased a fixed Christmas week time-share oceanfront condo in Princeville, Hawaii, for only $2,500, despite the fact that they are still selling these time-shares for $29,000 through the retail channel. Due to the demand for this unit, I'm able to trade it for three weeks in the Caribbean each year.

Remember, the goal is to gain financial freedom without having to restrict our lifestyles. Discovering how to buy more for less is consistent with this goal. Make this a game and have fun trying to save money!

Chapter Takeaway
Almost everything we buy can be purchased for a lower price. Searching for ways to save money without sacrificing quality can become a fun activity in and of itself. Make finding ways to save money on our purchases a challenging and entertaining game. It should be something like completing a crossword puzzle, except the reward is more satisfying, as it may be an extra vacation or adding to your freedom account.

Chapter 9
Debt Is a Four-Letter Word

Debt is the greatest irritant to our financial well-being. We've all seen bumper stickers that jokingly say, "I owe, I owe, so off to work I go." Unfortunately, this sad existence is how most consumers live their lives. We have become slaves to our debt and are frequently unable to pursue riskier and more fulfilling career paths because of our debt loads. Sometimes we can't even afford to satisfy our basic needs because of our debt loads.

How did this happen? When did it become okay to borrow money?

If we ask people how much they can afford to pay for a new car, most of them will respond with a monthly payment amount. In fact, many people who just purchased a car can't state the purchase price or the interest rate they are paying. All they know or care about are their monthly payments. Many people buy based on what the payments are. This is absurd.

We have been stupefied into believing that being in debt is the normal state we should expect.

While filling my tank at a gas station, a nearby customer complimented me on my car and asked politely what my monthly payments were. When I explained that I had no payments, he didn't understand. With a confused look, he asked me if I had won the car in a contest. I had to explain to him that I owned it free and clear because I had paid cash for it. I don't think he believed me.

Why did he assume that I had payments on my car? Why was it hard for him to grasp that I did not have payments? Had this person never owned a car free and clear?

The answer is that Madison Avenue advertising executives have brainwashed us again. They can persuade us to buy more by convincing us that it's okay, even normal, to buy on credit. They sidestep the affordability issue by focusing on "easy" monthly installments. Therefore, we have been bombarded with advertising that talks about monthly payments instead of the purchase price.

The interest they collect on the resulting debt can add up to more than the profit they make on the product they sold to us in the first place.

Corporations can more than double their profits by having us pay interest on our purchases.

Debt has become a huge industry. I probably receive ten unwanted solicitations in the mail each week with a credit card offer. This is a testament to how big and how profitable the debt industry has become.

The debt industry thrives due to our bad judgments regarding unwise and unaffordable purchases. They are parasites thriving because of our inappropriate decisions. They live off our suffering. In the past, their activities were in violation of usury laws. Maybe we should reenact these laws.

We must learn to live within our means, because it is simply impossible to get ahead if we are laden with debt.

Let's examine the cause and effects of debt. Let's assume that we have no extra money available. However, Madison Avenue has convinced us that we need another product and that it's okay to borrow money to buy this item. Since we have given control of our minds and money to Madison Avenue, we purchase the item using credit.

The following month we'll still need to buy the regular necessary items, but now we will have less money to purchase these items due to additional debt payments. The next month, once again advertising convinces us to buy something else that we don't need on credit. This could continue with the monthly debt toll growing, taking more of our cash each month, until we need to borrow money just to buy our basic needs. If we need to buy it on credit, we cannot afford it!

If we can't afford to pay cash, how can we afford to pay both the cash and the interest cost? Does adding interest cost make it more affordable?

We must learn to think about purchases in terms of how they affect our net worth, not just our monthly payments. Our net worth is the current market value of all our possessions less all our debt. We build financial freedom by growing our net worth.

Most things we buy are depreciating or wasting assets. Depreciating assets are items that are worth less each year. Depreciating assets include cars, furniture, clothes, TVs, computers, cell phones, electronics, and other items that lose value over time. Wasting assets include consumable items that disappear as we use them. Wasting assets include groceries, toiletries, gasoline, utilities, dining out, and most entertainment items.

Let's examine how buying on credit affects our net worth. Assume we buy a cell phone for $100 using a credit card since we can't afford to pay cash. Now let's look five years in the future. If we have a higher interest rate credit card (say about 18%) and we pay it off over five years, we would have paid about $45 in interest. At this point we would be hard-pressed to sell the five-year-old cell phone for $10 on Ebay. Let's examine our net worth at the five-year point. We own an item worth $10, less the $100 we paid for it, less the $45 we paid in interest. Thus, the effect of our purchase is negative $135 to our net worth. Without the debt, the effect would have only been negative $90.

Never buy a depreciating asset using debt.

When is it okay to incur debt? The answer is only when we are purchasing an appreciating asset, and even then we shouldn't use too much debt leverage. Let's assume that we are purchasing a home for $100,000. Let's also assume we borrow 70% ($70,000) of the purchase price using a 6.5% interest-only mortgage. Further, let's assume housing in our area appreciates an average of 5% a year over the next five years. At the end of five years, the home would have appreciated to $127,628, and we would have paid $22,750 in interest. The $27,628 appreciation has amounted to more than the $22,750 in interest charges, so there is a positive effect to our net worth. However, if we had borrowed 90% ($90,000) of the purchase price, our interest charges would have been $29,250. This amount is more than our appreciation, making the house purchase and mortgage a bad investment.

In summary, we should only use debt to purchase appreciating assets and never use debt for depreciating purchases.

Now this doesn't mean that we should go out and borrow money to purchase baseball cards or other illiquid collectible items we believe are appreciating. These are only hobbies for most people and therefore should not be supported by debt.

I am often asked if people should pay off their mortgages and own their houses free and clear. For most people this is a bad idea. The reason is the need for diversity. All or most of our assets should not be concentrated in one type of investment, particularly if that investment is illiquid like real estate. Remember, real estate (like the stock market) has risks and does not always go up in value. Further, not all risks are covered by insurance. As an example, a terrorist event or nuclear power plant accident could make the area's real estate worthless and is not covered by insurance.

Only pay off a home if the value is less than 20% of the family's total net worth. In other words, share the risk of real estate depreciation with your bank or mortgage company.

Liquidity, safety, and diversity could be improved if we maintain a low-interest-rate, tax-deductible mortgage and we invest the excess cash in an appropriate investment portfolio. The returns on the investments can be used to make the mortgage payments.

Okay, enough said about the evils of debt! Let's assume that we have succumbed to the billions of dollars Madison Avenue has spent convincing us to go into debt. After flogging ourselves repeatedly for getting into this situation, how do we get out of debt?

We can't have freedom and independence if we're enslaved by debt. We must begin by postponing plans to start a freedom account. Debt is the larger issue that must be addressed first.

There can be no freedom when shackled by debt!

Most of us have our heads in the sand regarding our debt situations. But in this position, we are leaving one natural target: our rear ends. Remember that image as you ignore your debt issues.

Let's start by getting our heads out of the sand. Ignoring the problem won't make it go away. Gather all financial statements and tally all debt exclusive of the mortgage. Remember the lessons of Business Management 101: "We can't improve it until we measure it." Don't forget to total all debt each month thereafter until it is all paid off. Tracking our progress will improve our motivation and results.

If the total debt is less than half of our annual income, we will probably be able to pay it off in three years. Just like it is possible to divert 20% to 25% of our annual income to our freedom accounts, it is possible to divert 20% to 25% of our income to paying off debt. Use the techniques taught in this book for finding 20% to 25% extra to first pay off debt before we start contributing to the freedom account.

Now use the basic needs budget shown in chapter 7 to determine how much money can be diverted to rapidly paying off debt. Use the tips shown in chapters 5 and 6 to control spending. Review chapter 8 to find areas ripe for saving. It may be necessary to make major housing and transportation cost reductions that chapters 10, 11, and 14 can help facilitate.

It is impossible to get ahead if we continue to finance the excesses of our previous lifestyle through debt. Zero debt is a prerequisite to financial health and success. Debt should be thought of as a disease. Just like cancer, debt must be cut from our lives. But, as a disease, debt is more like alcoholism in that we never get over the desire – we must learn to completely disallow debt in our lives. Just like alcoholism, oftentimes people live in denial that they even have this disease. We must recognize it and deal with the problem. The elimination of debt needs to be painful enough and hurtful enough that we will never allow ourselves to amass debt again. The twelve-step group called Debtors Anonymous (DA) offers moral support in our fight with the disease of debt. Find a local DA chapter on the web.

Remember, debt is a toxic disease that will ruin us if it continues. We need to make painful spending cuts that will not be forgotten. The fear of having to repeat these cuts should keep us from going into debt in the future. Give up cable and sell the large-screen TV. Give up all "wants". Sell the boat, the motorcycle, the luxury car, any collectibles, and jewelry. Forget buying clothing or going on vacation until the debt is paid off. Again, the sting of these cuts should hurt so much that they leave a lasting impression on our psyche.

This approach may seem harsh. However, the use of debt is an addictive disease with some characteristics similar to alcoholism. Would we ask an alcoholic to stop drinking every other day? Addiction to debt must be treated the same way. We must stop cold turkey and remove all debt from our lives as quickly and fully as possible. Madison Avenue advertising executives have taught us to use debt. Let's retake control of our lives and think for ourselves.

Remember, the sacrifices we are making now are short-term. The only permanent effect is learning not to abuse debt or credit. The pleasures of life should all be restored in just a few years, along with a new pleasure: *financial serenity*.

There is no such thing as "easy payments" - which is a Madison Avenue term designed to mislead us. Making payments and taking on debt is the path to personal financial collapse.

Madison Avenue has convinced us to use debt to buy things we cannot afford, and they convince us that we can afford more if we just make "easy payments." However, in reality, just the opposite is true. Once we start going into debt, we can afford less due to the debt payments. This begins a cycle in which every time we take on more debt we have less available for our basic needs. This can result in financial ruin. We must learn to associate debt with the pain of losing all we have. Our reaction should be serious. If it requires debt, just don't buy it!

There should never again be any pleasure in buying anything using credit or debt.

There should be a different sense of pleasure in owning something that is paid for than something that is not. Only a sense of guilt should come from buying something on credit. If it's paid for, you really do own it. If you used credit, you really don't own it.

Tracking debt and the progress of paying it off is important. Ignoring how much our balances were growing is likely what got us into deep debt in the first place. It is nearly impossible to repair our debt problems without close monitoring. What we don't measure we can't fix. To get out of debt, we must tally our total debt each month. Continue this every month until the total is zero. There is an Excel spreadsheet available to help you with this at www.poor-no-more.com.

Sometimes it's possible to find ways to lower interest payments on debt. Call creditors and explain that you are in trouble and need help. They often have programs that can help. Sometimes creditors work with agencies that negotiate with all our creditors to lower the interest rates on outstanding debt.

Be aware that there are many companies masquerading as credit counselors that are just attempting to get us to consolidate our debt with them. These firms will offer some reductions in monthly payment amounts. However, these payment reductions come at the terrible expense of longer terms. Staying in debt longer is not our goal. Our goal is to get out of debt as soon as possible. Remember, agreeing to make payments is what got us into this problem in the first place. Don't go from one problem to another. Quit thinking in terms of payments; instead, think in terms of the total debt outstanding. The goal is to remove the debt, not just reduce payments.

Loan consolidation is acceptable only if the term is short (less than three years) and at a very low interest rate. Do not simply go for a lower payment.

The goal is to reduce total debt, not just the dollar amount of the monthly payments.

Homeowners may also consider using a second mortgage to pay off debts. Second mortgages may be tax-deductible and have lower interest rates. However, do not get a line of credit that allows borrowing more. Remember, paying off debt should be a painful experience that is not forgotten. The term should be fixed with no more than a three-year payoff. The second mortgage should not be more than the total of all debt - don't take cash out of your home. The loan should amortize over three years with principal and interest payments. An interest-only loan or a loan with a balloon payment does not solve the debt problem. It only reduces the payments and postpones the problem. Remember, we are trying to get out of debt, not add to it. Paying debt off is the goal. Not just another loan.

If your total debt is above 50% of your annual income, consider bankruptcy. If done properly, a respectable credit score can be obtained again within five years. However, it will be ten years before the bankruptcy is off your credit record. The good news is that bankruptcy will remove all debt and prevent you from using credit for the next few years.

Think of debt as vermin in your house that you must eradicate. It is impossible to have financial serenity in the presence of debt.

Chapter Takeaway

Madison Avenue advertising executives have brainwashed us again, convincing us that it is okay and normal to buy on credit. They sidestep the affordability issue by focusing on "easy" monthly installments. There is no such thing as "easy payments." If we can't afford to pay cash, how can we afford to pay both the cash and the interest cost? Does adding interest cost make it more affordable? Making payments and taking on debt is the path to personal financial collapse.

We have been stupefied into believing that debt is the normal state we should expect to be in. Debt is not normal! Debt is the greatest irritant to our financial well-being. The only solution is to *never* buy on credit.

Chapter 10
Cars: Budget Sucking Machines

The American love affair with cars, trucks, and SUVs is out of control. Expenditures on these vehicles can often reach 30%, 40%, or even 50% of people's incomes. It is impossible for people to gain lasting wealth if they divert such a large percentage of their incomes into depreciating assets, worth nothing in a few years, like automobiles.

The logic, or rather, "illogic," people use when making their transportation choices is nonsensical. Auto finance companies will qualify car loan payments of up to 50% of an individual's income. Because they qualify, people think the car is affordable. We must learn to differentiate the ability "to qualify for" from the ability "to afford" a purchase. What we can qualify for is the car dealership's decision based on their greedy motivation to sell us a car. What we can afford should be our decision based on the detailed budget we have developed. See chapter 7.

I have devoted two chapters in this book to transportation issues because this is where most people blow their budgets, bury themselves in debt, and prevent the possibility of ever being debt-free or having financial freedom. Stop the insanity!

Madison Avenue has completely convinced us that our image and self-worth is all wrapped up in the car selection we make. "We are what we drive" is the idea they want us to believe. Therefore, we end up buying cars we can't possibly afford in order to feel good about ourselves. Once again we have surrendered our minds to Madison Avenue.

Do we actually feel better about ourselves because of the car we are driving, or is it because of the brainwashing we've been subjected to on TV? Some aspects of a car may make it more comfortable - the ride, the seats, the climate control, etc. However, the style, make, and model do not affect our true comfort. Yet, due to Madison Avenue, many of us feel depressed and have low self-esteem if we are driving an older economy car. Get over it! Let's start thinking for ourselves!

A car provides transportation and is not a symbol of our self-worth. Establish financial freedom if personal validation is needed.

Young men will buy exotic cars in order to impress women. Have these young men thought about what it means if a woman is only interested in your car, not in you? If it makes a difference to the lady what car is being driven, then find a different lady.

I have heard several salesmen say they need a late-model luxury car in order to impress their clients. The logic is, if we're selling success, then we need to look successful ourselves. However, as someone in the financial advisory business, I know that this is an overstatement enforced by Madison Avenue. Of course it would be difficult to sell financial advice standing on a freeway exit ramp holding a sign that said, "I give financial advice for food." In certain professions, it is unwise to appear poor. However, obtaining the appearance of being well-off shouldn't have to make us poor. This chapter and chapter 11 will provide techniques to buy an affordable car that will meet these needs.

What we qualify for is not the same as what we can afford.

Most people have no idea what they can afford when it comes to a car. They haven't completed a personal budget, which provides the information needed to determine what can be afforded. So what do they do? They allow the car salesman and his finance guy to determine what they can qualify for, and then falsely assume this is what they can afford. Do these guys have our best interests at heart? Do these guys even ask about other financial issues? Are they concerned about our savings for financial independence? Let's start thinking for ourselves!

Despite the obvious conflict of interest, many of us allow the car finance guy to decide what we can and cannot afford. As a result of this, many of us spend too much on transportation. Our transportation costs should be capped at about 10% of our after-tax income. However, since loan-qualifying ratios (the percentage of our payments versus our take-home income) are as high as 30%, some of us spend 30% or more on transportation. This is ridiculous! Remember, cars are depreciating assets; therefore, we need to minimize our exposure.

Would we buy more of a stock if we knew it was going to drop in value? Yet, people are proud to spend more on expensive cars that they know for certain are going down in value. What is the logic of this?

Limiting our exposure to depreciating assets is an absolute requirement for gaining financial freedom. Again, we need to cap our monthly payments for transportation costs to about 10% of our after-tax income. Furthermore, we should cap the value or purchase cost of all our vehicles to about 25% of our take-home annual income. These limits will eliminate new car purchases for some buyers.

These limits may be hard to swallow. However, it is a mathematical certainty that if we don't enforce these limits, we will never get ahead in life! The budget examples at the end of chapter 7 show that there is no room in our budgets for additional transportation costs.

We must choose between growing financial independence and rapidly depreciating automobiles.

I know a construction worker who was making good money by his standards. His friend and co-worker bought a new, fully loaded, pickup truck. Not to be outdone, this construction worker "had to" purchase a top-of-the-line pickup with every possible option. Then he spent another $12,000 to have his truck custom "lifted." This included special steps that automatically folded out as the door opened. This allowed people to step up into this ridiculously high truck. The construction worker loved his "cool" truck. However, the payments were 21% of his take-home monthly pay, and the total purchase price was 45% of his take-home annual pay.

Within a year, the shimmer of the new truck was starting to fade. The construction worker wanted to also own a new Corvette. After all, his brother-in-law had one. Madison Avenue had taken over his mind!

The dealership finance man explained to the construction worker that he could qualify if he made a large enough down payment and stretched the payments over seventy-two months, but the interest rate would be a little higher.

Again, what we can qualify for and what we can afford are not the same thing. Dealerships want us to buy regardless of our ability to pay, and therefore will find a way to make it happen. Qualifying ratios are ridiculously high, allowing us to buy cars we can't afford.

When a dealership finance guy suggests we should make a larger down payment, a red light should turn on in our heads. He needs the larger down payment because it is likely we can't afford the car, and he wants protection from losses if he needs to repossess it later. This request should give us cause to pause. A second red light should turn on when the dealership suggests stretching the payment period. This indicates that we don't meet the qualifying ratio. A third red light should turn on when the dealership says a higher interest rate will be required. This indicates that the loan is high risk and our chance of default is high. Why would we risk financial ruin for a car?

As a rule of thumb ask the dealership if we would qualify on a twenty-four-month payment plan. If the answer is no, then we probably can't afford the car. I'm not saying we should finance the car for only twenty-four months, but if the dealership won't qualify us for the shorter term, we can't afford the purchase. In truth, there is no substitute for doing the budget planning as described in chapter 7 and determining for ourselves if we can afford the car.

Well, the construction worker ignored the red lights and bought the Corvette. His wife was very upset about the purchase. Within three months he realized he could not afford both vehicles, and he tried to sell the pickup. Due to the pickup's rapid depreciation and his need for a quick sell, he had to considerably drop the price.

After a week and no offers, he decided to drop the price another $3,000. The next day, his wife announced she was two months' pregnant. When we don't plan for or allow for the unexpected to happen, it will always happen at the worst possible time.

Another week passed without an offer, so he dropped the price another $2,000. That afternoon he was laid off from his construction job. Within a week the wife had moved out and filed for divorce, citing her husband's lack of financial responsibility. The divorce papers said she was suing for alimony and child support for the yet-unborn children. Did I mention the ultrasound indicated twins?

Okay, I made up the part about the twins, and I know that this scenario sounds like the lyrics for a country and western song. Yet every day this scenario plays out hundreds of times across America.

We must think and budget for ourselves before we make a major purchase!

There is no substitute for developing a budget and determining for ourselves what we can afford. Let's think for ourselves! If we allow the car dealership to think for us, we would be better served just giving the money to a good charity.

The purchase cost is not the only cost of owning a vehicle. Operational costs include annual title/property tax, insurance, gasoline, maintenance, and repairs. As a rule of thumb our purchase-related costs should be about 10% of our monthly income while our operating costs should total another 3% of monthly income.

Before buying a car, consider all of the related operating costs. Estimate gasoline costs by multiplying the number of miles driven each month by the MPG rating. If we have a long commute, this can be more than the purchase cost. Get quotes on insurance rates. These rates vary a great deal by the model you choose. Sports cars will generally have the highest rates. Always consider insurance cost before finalizing the purchase.

Repair and maintenance costs will generally be higher for used cars. However, these costs will often be offset by lower insurance cost, lower sales taxes, and lower title taxes. We need to determine and calculate all these factors before making an intelligent purchase decision. It is impossible to complete these calculations on a dealership's lot. Don't make a spontaneous purchase - examine all of the costs before buying.

Car dealerships normally attempt to close the deal the first time we step onto the lot. We will hear noise from them such as "You will never get as good of a deal as today," followed by some ridiculous reason why. Don't believe it. Buy a car only when you are ready and all evaluations are completed. Make an informed choice and turn a deaf ear to the noise coming out of the car salesman's mouth.

Do your homework and complete a budget before buying. Know all ownership costs.

Also study the dealer's cost. If buying a new car, log on to the Kelley Blue Book at www.kbb.com and look up the dealer's invoice cost for the vehicle. Generally, we can buy the car for close to this invoice price. Keep in mind that dealers often pay less than the invoice cost due to their volume discounts.

If you are buying a used car, also go to www.kbb.com, and enter the make, model, options, and mileage. Normally you can buy the car for around the private party price.

I've noticed that I can get a better deal on a car on the last day of the month (this is probably due to monthly quotas). So does this mean we should go shopping on the last day of the month? The answer is no. We should do our shopping, research, and home study about a car leading up to the last day of the month. Then go back on the last day when the salesmen are determined to close the deal.

Chapter Takeaway

Our obsession with automobiles causes many people to blow their budgets and bury themselves in debt, and prevents the possibility of ever being debt-free or having financial freedom. Expenditures on vehicles can reach insane levels of 50% of income. It is impossible for people to gain lasting wealth if they divert such a large percentage of their income into depreciating assets, worth nothing in a few years. We must choose between growing financial independence and rapidly depreciating automobiles. We must learn that what we qualify for is not the same as what we can afford. We must learn how to think and budget for ourselves before we make a major purchase.

People's transportation choices have become nonsensical. Madison Avenue has completely convinced us that our image and self-worth are all wrapped up in the car selection we make. "We are what we drive" is the slogan they promote. A car provides transportation and is not a symbol of our self-worth. Establish financial freedom if personal validation is needed.

When considering buying a car, remember that Madison Avenue advertising executives are whispering in our ears without our conscious knowledge of their existence. When buying a car to improve our self-worth, remember that the car will depreciate, eventually reducing our financial self-worth. The only way to add lasting wealth to our lives is to buy appreciating assets, not depreciating assets like automobiles. Let's reduce our appetite for automobiles to reasonable levels.

Chapter 11
You Versus Car Dealerships

Let's admit it. Car dealerships are crafty, and they are happy to separate us from our money. Their massive advertising campaigns are designed to make us believe their hype. This has been going on for multiple generations, so their lies have become rooted in our belief system.

So, what is the biggest lie that car salesmen will tell? Here is their classic lie: "It's not the cost of the car that's important; it's the amount of the payments." This is an absurd statement, but it's been told for so long that people believe it. So if we change the loan payments from thirty-six months to seventy-two months, has the cost of the car gone down as much as the payments? How ridiculous it would be to think that! Increasing the number of months just increases our total interest cost and total purchase price.

The cost of a car is not the cost of the monthly payments!

Many people incorrectly equate the cost of their cars with the amount of their payments. The payments are a measure of the interest rate, the number of months financed, and the down payment amount. Payments do not equate to the cost. Our true costs are much different when properly viewed.

What is the true cost of borrowing money? Is it simply the cost of our loan payments? The answer is no! Part of the payment repays the loan balance. This part of the payment relieves the liability we have for money we are using. The other part is interest, which represents the bank's profit. The interest part is our true cost.

To better understand, let's consider what happens if we borrow $20,000 cash. If our loan terms are for thirty-six months at 7% interest, our monthly payment will be $613.96. Out of that payment, our average interest cost is $58.40. So does this loan cost us $613.96 per month? The correct cost is only the interest cost, $58.40, because the remainder of the payment reduces our debt.

The same is true for car loan payments. The majority of the payments simply reduces debt and adds to our ownership of the car. Somehow people forget this fact and how our ownership is building up. In the example above, the $20,000 loan proceeds remained in the bank without losing any value. In the case of a car, the value is decreasing, which camouflages our increasing ownership in the car. The highest cost of car ownership is the decreasing value, or depreciation, which has no relationship to the fixed monthly payments.

The largest cost of car ownership is the depreciation!

Since depreciation is the largest cost of car ownership, estimating the amount of future depreciation should be the paramount issue when selecting a car.

As I stated in chapter 9, the true cost of a purchase is not the purchase price or the payments; it is instead how the purchase affects net worth over the length of ownership. In the case of a depreciating asset, such as a car, the largest cost of ownership is the value depreciation over the time of ownership. Costs of car ownership include depreciation cost, sales tax, and interest expenses. Costs of car operation include annual title/property tax, insurance, gasoline, maintenance, and repairs.

Let's first examine ownership cost. Notice that the above list does not include the purchase price or the monthly payment amount, which are the two items most people evaluate in order to determine if they can afford a car.

Let me explain how to properly evaluate a car purchase. As I previously stated, the largest cost of ownership is the depreciating value of the car. To calculate this, add the sales tax to the purchase price and then subtract your projected selling price when disposing of the car. The results equal the total depreciation cost. Now, divide this figure by the number of months projected to own the car e.g., 24, 36, 48, or 60. The result is the monthly depreciation cost.

Let's take the example of buying a new Chevrolet Impala four-door LS sedan (with only the standard LS options) and keeping it for three years. Further, let's assume we have good credit and can get a 7% loan for three years with no money down.

According to Kelley Blue Book (as of October 4, 2006), we can expect to pay $20,071 for this car (which is about $1,000 less than the MSRP). We now need to add the 8% sales tax ($1,605) to our purchase price, thus totaling $21,676.

Log on to Kelley Blue Book (www.kbb.com) to discover what the value should be when we sell the car in three years. Click on "used cars," click on "2003," then "Chevrolet," then "Impala LS four-door," and enter "36,000" as the mileage (12,000 per year). Let's further assume we don't smoke in the car or have kids who trash the backseat, or that we live in the northeast where road salt deteriorates the finish, so that we can enter the condition as "good."

After completing the above, the Kelley site returns a private party (if we sold it ourselves) value of $11,710. This will be the projected selling price when we dispose of the car.

We now subtract the projected sale price of $11,710 at the end of three years from the total purchase price of $21,676. This results in a total value depreciation of $9,967 - that is the difference between the two values. If we divide this $9,967 by the 36 months we plan on owning the car, our monthly depreciation costs are $277 per month.

Notice that the cost of sales tax has been added to your purchase price and thus is fully accounted for in the monthly depreciation cost of the car. Also notice that the down payment amount and loan terms do not affect the depreciation cost. However, both of these items have large effects on our monthly loan payments. Depreciation costs are only affected by the value decline curve. This decline curve can be estimated by using www.kbb.com as shown above.

The true monthly purchase cost of a car is the average monthly value decrease plus the average monthly interest costs.

The decline curve varies a great deal based on the make and model. Thus, shopping for the best deal may have less to do with shopping for the best price and more to do with searching Kelley Blue Book to find the make and model with the flattest decline curve.

Returning to our example, if we finance the purchase price of $20,071 for three years at a 7% interest rate, our payments will be about $616.14 per month. This totals to $22,181 ($616.14 times 36 months). The difference between our total payments and our total amount financed ($20,071) is our total finance cost, in this case $2,110. Note: The car's purchase statement will also disclose total finance cost. If we divide this by 36 months, we derive our average monthly interest cost of $58.61.

The purchase cost is $277 per month in depreciation, plus $59 per month in interest, totaling $336 per month. This $336 per-month figure is our true ownership cost. Notice how different this amount is from our monthly payment of $616.

How can our cost of ownership be so much less than our payment? It is because our higher monthly payment is largely a payment to ourselves in the form of increasing equity ownership in the car.

Now let's change the terms of the loan to a 7% interest rate for five years instead of three years. How will this affect our monthly payment and our monthly cost of ownership?

Our monthly payment will drop to $395. However, our monthly cost of ownership will barely change, increasing from $336 to $368. How is this possible? Our depreciation cost remains at $277 per month and is not affected by our loan terms. Our total interest cost will go up slightly from $59 to $61 per month due to the longer term.

Stretching the loan term from thirty-six months to sixty months may reduce monthly payments by 35%, but this will actually slightly increase the monthly cost of ownership.

How can the cost of ownership remain nearly the same when the payment drops so much? The lower monthly payment simply reduces the rate of debt reduction, so that at the end of three years we will have less ownership or equity.

Is it better to lease or buy a new car?
Many people believe it is cheaper to lease a car than to buy it. I often get asked if it is better to purchase or to lease a car. My response to this question begins with my own question: Do you believe in Santa Claus and the Tooth Fairy? This question isn't as silly as it seems, because what I am really asking is if you believe that car dealerships would spend money advertising a payment plan that costs less and gives them less profit. Not likely!

By examining lease payment amounts, we will discover that, at best, these lease payments equal the average monthly depreciation cost plus the monthly interest cost. Therefore, lease deals offer no advantages. Frequently, these plans also assume far too few miles will be driven and charge too much for extra miles. These plans often have very restrictive early termination fees. As in most "good deals," the devil is in the details, and it's easy to miss some of these details. In short, stay away from these plans. They are money traps favoring the car dealerships.

Tax accountants like to discuss the pros and cons of leasing when the car is used for business purposes. If we lease, we can deduct the leasing costs as a business expense. If we purchase, we can deduct the interest costs and depreciation costs as a business expense. Either way the total deductions are about the same. If an accountant can find a way that leasing has a small tax advantage, it is not likely that this advantage will outweigh the flexibility of owning.

Is it better to buy new or used cars?
The answer depends on the price decline curve of the car selected. Some models decline rapidly within the first few years and then level off. For these models, buying a three-year-old car and keeping it three years can be far less expensive than a new car.

Other models keep a steady dollar value decline over many years. For these models, we may want to buy new. The point of this chapter is to provide the tools to make this evaluation.

To assess buying new versus buying used, let's return to our Chevrolet Impala four-door LS sedan. According to www.kbb.com, the private party purchase price of a two-year-old (2004) model with 24,000 miles is $13,515. Similarly, we project what we can sell this car for three years later by looking up the

2001 model year prices for the same car with 60,000 miles. The private party "good condition" price is $8,705. If we add an 8% sales tax to our $13,515 purchase price, to total $14,596, and then subtract the projected selling price of $8,705, we can calculate our total depreciation to be $5,643. By dividing by 36 months, this gives us a depreciation cost of $164 per month. This is far less than the $277 cost for the new Impala.

Do these cost trends hold up for all cars? The answer is no. Decline curves are very sensitive to make and model. Let's review a few examples: the Toyota Camry LE four-door sedan automatic 4-cylinder, the BMW 325ci coupe, and the Mercedes ML350 SUV.

The table below is for a three-year ownership period starting new or in year two, three, or four. From this table, we see that it is clearly less expensive to purchase a two-year-old Impala or Mercedes ML350. However, the other two cars have a more constant decline curve with little advantage to buying an older car.

I have also included a table that examines the cost of ownership if we only keep the car for two years. Two-year monthly depreciation costs are much higher. This is due to there being less time for the decline curve to flatten, and because there is less time to amortize the sales tax cost. I recommend holding a car at least three years. Five years is much better.

Three-Year Ownership Period Average Monthly Price Decline (Depreciation)

Model (Purchase Price)	Buying New	Buying Two Years Old	Buying Three Years Old	Buying Four Years Old
Toyota Camry ($18,854 new)	$210	$202	$182	$171
Chevrolet Impala ($20,071 new)	$277	$164	$159	$157
BMW 325ci coupe ($31,329 new)	$307	$323	$289	$231
Mercedes ML350 ($38,120 new)	$526	$329	$299	$262

Note that in the above examples, information was taken from the Kelley Blue Book on October 5, 2006. At another point in time, the information will be different. Further, information will vary depending on ZIP code.

But relax; there is no need to do the boring math. I have made an Excel spreadsheet to help. Just log on to www.poor-no-more.com and download the spreadsheet.

Two-Year Ownership Period Average Monthly Price Decline (Depreciation)

Model (Purchase Price)	Buying New	Buying Two Years Old	Buying Three Years Old	Buying Four Years Old
Toyota Camry ($18,854 new)	$243	$191	$225	$199
Chevrolet Impala ($20,071 new)	$340	$185	$164	$168
BMW 325ci coupe ($31,329 new)	$338	$367	$351	$263
Mercedes ML350 ($38,120 new)	$654	$373	$347	$284

Should I finance my car purchase or pay cash?

The previous chapters of this book explained my preference to avoid debt. The feeling of being debt-free is far more important than the joy of a new car. Debt is a bad habit, and debt is always dangerous. However, this book is about financial reality and not about my feelings regarding debt. So, is debt a bad thing when it comes to cars?

The answer is, from a purely financial net worth viewpoint, not always. It depends on the circumstances and our credit rating. As an example, if we had plenty of money invested, let's say several times more than the cost of the car, it is okay to reduce our investments and pay cash for the car. However, we would be losing the financial return (gain) we should have been making on the investments. On the other hand, we would be saving the interest cost on our car payment. From a mathematical viewpoint, if our car payment interest rate is lower than our expected investment rate of return, then we should keep the cash in the investment and use a loan to purchase the car. However, if our credit score is bad and our car purchase interest rate is high, the reverse is true. We would be better off paying cash and avoiding the high interest charges.

If we have a bad credit score, all purchases are difficult. Let's return to the Chevy Impala example, where we assumed we had good credit and were financing $20,071 for three years, and a 7% interest rate was possible. Our total payment was $619, and our average interest charge was $58 per month. Interest payments amounted to only 9% of the total payment.

If we had a bad credit score, the interest rate could be as high as 18%. This would change our three-year payments to $715 per month. This higher payment could drive us to finance for five years. Thus payments would be reduced to $502, including the average monthly interest charges of $166.62. Over the life of the loan, almost $10,000, or a third of the payments, would go to paying interest. Therefore, we should avoid debt and pay cash.

However, many of us will not have enough money to pay cash. What should we do? A good option would be to buy a lower-mileage, seven-year-old economy car for cash equal to about what a down payment would be on a new car. We can drive this car for the next eighteen months while saving the equivalent of the payments being avoided in a special account earmarked for the next car purchase. If the payments would have been $400, we would save $7,200 over the eighteen months.

At the end of the eighteen month period, we sell the older car (which will not have depreciated much) and add the $7,200 we have saved to buy a much nicer and newer used car. After repeating this cycle one more time, we will be driving a nice late-model car with no debt.

Notice that with this last approach, a person just starting out or with bad credit can soon own (free and clear) a late-model car with no debt. How can this happen in such a short period of only three years? It's because this person avoids interest payments and the faster depreciation of a new car.

The above example points to the larger lessons of personal finance.

We can get almost everything we want if we use patience instead of debt and credit.

Before buying a car, I suggest we review the total cost of owning and operating the car. To do this, complete the following table:

Total Cost of Owning an Automobile

Monthly depreciation cost   _____

Monthly interest cost   _____

Annual title tax divided by 12	_____
Monthly insurance cost	_____
Monthly gasoline cost	_____
Monthly maintenance cost	_____
Monthly repair cost	_____

Remember to evaluate all the costs of ownership for each car model you are considering before making a purchase decision. You cannot expect to be able to do this on a car dealership lot. Ignore the car salesman asking if you are ready to make a decision "today." Walking away will only make the dealer more price-flexible the next day. Take time to make the decision. Most of these ownership costs will vary significantly from model to model. Do the homework before you buy. Purchasing a car is a major decision and should not be an impulse purchase.

Due to the increased cost of gasoline, should I trade my car for a hybrid or more fuel-efficient car?

Often we will find that it doesn't make sense to change cars just to lower our gasoline costs. It usually makes more sense to wait until we were planning to change anyway.

If you want to evaluate making such a change, complete the Total Cost of Owning an Automobile table for both your current car and the fuel-efficient car being considered. If your total cost of ownership is less with the fuel-efficient car, then make the change. The rule is: Don't just trust your gut feeling on which is more economical; do the math and consider all the costs. Included in the web site www.poor-no-more.com, I have included an Excel spreadsheet that will aid you in completing the necessary math to determine the correct course of action.

Chapter Takeaway

Does changing the loan payments from thirty-six months to seventy-two months reduce the cost of a car? The answer is no – it simply reduces the monthly payments. In fact, increasing the number of months just increases our total interest cost and total purchase price. The cost of a car is not the cost of the monthly payments!

The true cost of a car includes interest cost, operating cost, and the value the car depreciates during our ownership. We must learn how to properly evaluate the true cost of car ownership so that we can make proper purchase decisions.

Chapter 12
How Did I Blow All That?

Wealthy people, or soon-to-be-wealthy people, have a different way of thinking about money. They understand the simple concept that money is something to hold on to and safely invest. Wealthy people are accustomed to having and building cash and investments. This is what makes them wealthy! They feel no need to spend cash windfalls when they occur. Lump sum cash windfalls provide just another opportunity to add to their wealth. In contrast, poor people, or soon-to-be-poor people, will quickly spend their cash windfalls - typically on items that add no lasting benefit to their lives. These wasteful spending decisions are what makes them and keeps them poor!

It seems almost silly to have a chapter dedicated to such a simple concept. However, my years as a financial advisor have taught me that many people do not understand the importance of holding on to their cash windfalls. To some, it's like the cash in their hands is on fire - and must be immediately spent before it burns them. They must find some way to spend their new cash. They need to show off their new wealth to friends and family. Of course, by spending their wealth to show it off, they will no longer have their windfalls.

Most of us will experience some occurrence in our lives that offers an opportunity to permanently change our lives. By this I mean that a lump sum of cash falls our way. This could mean we collect a fat life insurance check; an inheritance comes our way; we sell a highly appreciated property; we collect a large reward from a lawsuit; we receive a divorce settlement; that trip to Vegas works out incredibly well; or we win a big state lottery - it could happen. The important question is: Will we still have the money three years later? Will the cash windfall make a long-term difference in our lives?

People do not properly contemplate the use of cash windfalls; an easy come, easy go attitude prevails.

All of the above occurrences represent an opportunity to permanently change our lives. As a practicing financial advisor, I often see money coming in from these events; however, I seldom see the recipients making positive long-term changes to their lives. Often, they rationalize why it's okay to spend some of the money. Here are some examples:

1) I really need a new car. My repair bills are too high. My car's not safe.
2) A new car or wardrobe will improve my image and business.
3) I work hard and need a break and a vacation.
4) I need to visit friends or family.
5) I need to help a family member. (By the way, this almost never works out.)

6) I am only going to spend 10% to 20% of the money I receive to treat myself.
7) I work hard; I deserve it. (My favorite rationalization.)

The above issues existed before the lump sum, and they will reoccur three years later, even if the newfound fortunes are spent on these issues. If we were able to cope with these concerns before we got the cash windfall, then why can't we cope with these concerns without spending that new chunk of cash? These issues are recurring and will reappear in the near future even if we blow our new fortune on them.

What is the most frequent waste of cash windfalls? As a financial advisor, I have seen these windfalls wasted in many ways, but the most common waste is a parent attempting to help their adult child. First of all, this almost never helps the child. It tends to only make adult children more dependent and less responsible for their own actions. It often causes friction and resentment between spouses. Finally, the help seldom has the desired lasting effect because it fails to teach the adult child about self-reliance. If you feel the overwhelming desire to give your adult children unsolicited advice, I suggest sending them a copy of this book.

Don't blow our cash windfalls.

The lump sum cash windfall can have lasting benefits to our lives only if we invest the money carefully. Interest and dividends from the invested lump sum can provide for extra monthly cash for the rest of our lives. This extra monthly cash could be used to address some of the previously listed "spending issues" on a long-term basis.

As a practicing financial advisor, I have often observed the following: If clients can rationalize spending some of their cash windfalls, they normally spend through all of them within three years. The only people who hold on to their cash windfalls are those who never touch even the smallest part of their new wealth. The lesson is, once we can rationalize using some of the money, we almost always end up spending it all. Don't blow it! Spending only the interest and dividends earned will provide us with extra income for the rest of our lives. Hang on to the money!

Spending our new fortunes on depreciating assets or on recurring issues will leave us with no permanent and lasting change in our lives.

It is vital that we hang on to our cash windfalls. And the only way to ensure this happens is to never spend any of it. No short-term reasons, excuses, or rationalizations will make a long-term change in our lives. Long-term change is only possible if we hang on to and safely invest the cash.

Chapter Takeaway
Once again, there is a significant difference between how wealthy people and poor people think. Wealthy people hold on to their cash and invest it wisely. This is what makes them wealthy! Poor people always find some reason to spend the cash - normally in a way that will make no lasting difference in their lives. This keeps them poor!

The future is not just now; it is the rest of our lives. Don't blow cash windfalls! Invest them in a way that will be beneficial for the rest of our lives. Why only benefit in the soon-to-be-forgotten short-term? Why not stretch our benefits for the rest of our lives and make a permanent difference?

Chapter 13
Proper Use and Control of Credit

Many people are ignorant of their credit status, and it often seems as though they don't believe they have the right to know their credit rating. They incorrectly believe that only banks or finance companies can view their credit information, or they just don't understand how to obtain and interpret available credit information about themselves. Possibly they have no idea how their actions affect their credit ratings. This chapter intends to address these issues.

Before we discuss what a credit score is and how it is determined, let's first look at why a credit rating is so important. An average American family can save $10,824 per year or $902 per month by increasing their FICO credit score from 560 to 760. This example assumes that the family has a $300,000 mortgage and two $25,000 car loans. This breaks down to a monthly mortgage savings of $686 and car loan savings of $108 each (two cars). Higher savings are possible with higher debt. Now does it make sense to learn about and manage FICO scores?

Table 13.1
Cost of a 30-Year $300,000 Home Mortgage*

FICO Score	Annual Percentage Rate	Higher APR Due to Lower FICO Score	Monthly Payment	Higher Payment Due to Lower FICO Score
760–850	6.108 %	0 %	$1,820	$0
700–759	6.329 %	0.221 %	$1,853	$33
660–699	6.613 %	0.505 %	$1,919	$99
620–659	7.421 %	1.313 %	$2,081	$260
580–619	8.976 %	2.868 %	$2,409	$589
500–579	9.423 %	3.315 %	$2,506	$686

* The above information was derived from www.myFICO.com on September 5, 2007, and is only an estimate subject to market changes.

The above $902 monthly savings resulted from a 200-point improvement in a FICO credit score. Such an improvement could take six months or more to accomplish. However, I have seen people make a 100-point improvement in their FICO credit scores in just thirty days. In the above example, a savings of $9,036 per year or $753 per month would result from increasing the FICO score from 560 to 660. This breaks down to monthly savings of $597 on the mortgage and $78 on each car loan. It makes sense to learn how you can improve your FICO credit score by 100 points.

Table 13.2
Cost of a 48-Month $25,000 Auto Loan*

FICO Score	Annual Percentage Rate	Higher APR Due to Lower FICO Score	Monthly Payment	Higher Payment Due to Lower FICO Score
760–850	7.200 %	0 %	$601	$0
700–759	8.088 %	0.888 %	$611	$10
660–699	9.783 %	2.583 %	$631	$30
620–659	11.586 %	4.386 %	$653	$52
580–619	14.944 %	7.744 %	$695	$94
500–579	16.012 %	8.812 %	$709	$108

* The above information was derived from www.myFICO.com on September 5, 2007, and is only an estimate subject to market changes.

Now that I've made the importance of our FICO scores clear, let's talk about how our credit history is tracked and reported, and how we can monitor and positively affect this important process. There are three major reporting agencies: Equifax, TransUnion, and Experian. They each keep files on every person, which may differ significantly among the three agencies. These files contain our credit history: including currently owed balance, maximum allowed balance, minimum payment requirement, and history of late payments.

All three of these companies will report our history to our creditors and to us if we request the report. They also report a summary credit score called a FICO score. The three reporting agencies have hired Fair Isaac Corporation to calculate this FICO score using the information from our credit history files. A FICO score can range between 300 and 850. The score represents Fair Isaac's estimate of the risk of someone missing a payment or defaulting on a loan. The higher the FICO score, the lower the risk we are to lenders and thus the lower the interest rate they will charge.

Notice that our income levels do not affect our FICO scores. In fact, race, religion, national origin, sex, marital status, age, occupation, job title, employer, employment history, where we live, family, and child support obligations are ignored when calculating our FICO scores. Part of the reason FICO scores are used is the perception that lending will be fairer if loan qualifying is based on a computer-based creditworthiness score. Be aware that many hiring employers will examine our FICO scores as a measure of our reliability. Even insurance companies will examine our FICO scores as they allege low FICO scores increase the likelihood of claims.

So how do we improve our FICO scores? The first step to improving our scores is to monitor our scores. This goes back to Business Management 101: We can't improve something until we measure it! There are many ways to obtain our credit reports. However, many of the free services, free websites, and other methods to obtain our reports can result in credit inquiries on our records that lower our FICO scores. Therefore, I recommend that we purchase a credit report for all three credit agencies though www.myFICO.com. This costs about $50 and will not count as a credit inquiry lowering our credit scores.

Table 13.3
FICO Score vs. Risk of Defaulting*

FICO Score	Risk of Defaulting
800 +	1 %
750–799	2 %
700–749	5 %
650–699	14 %
600–649	31 %
550–599	51 %
500–549	70 %
Below 500	83 %

*The above information was derived from www.myFICO.com as of September 5, 2007, and is only an estimate.

It is nearly impossible to improve our FICO scores if we are not routinely monitoring these scores!

Review all three reports in detail, looking for errors in the files. First review personal information such as name spelling, other names used, date of birth, social security number, previous addresses, current address, previous employers, and current employer, and ask each of the reporting agencies to make corrections as required. The reports include contact information and instructions for making corrections. Make certain that ex-spouses are not listed in the report. I have never seen a report that started with all of the above information correct. Be very certain that inappropriate names and unknown addresses are removed, as these could be the result of others attempting to use our credit or identity theft.

Second, review each debt shown in the report, looking for errors. Determine if the partial account numbers on the credit report align with the full account numbers on your statements. Does the balance shown match your latest statement? Does the maximum allowed limit match your latest statement? Are there any late payments shown, and are these reports correct? Often there will be debt listed that is not known to you. Tell the reporting agency that this information is not correct and ask them to remove the debt listing. If you have previous paid-off debt or other debt in good standing that is not shown on the credit report, follow the recommended steps to have it included in your history. This type of error is frequently caused by a creditor not having the correct social security number.

Now that we have corrected all the mistakes in our credit reports, it is time to take on improving our scores. This requires constant monitoring. I believe the best way to accomplish this is by purchasing a "Score Watch" from www.myFICO.com. This costs about $90 per year for a once-a-year purchase or $9 per month if we prefer. I have programmed this service to send e-mails and text my cell phone any time there is a credit inquiry, a new account, a debit balance change, or any changes to my FICO score. This way, I can monitor my progress on improving my credit score. A periodic review of our FICO scores is *not* sufficient. Active monitoring is needed, and this

"Score Watch" service fills that need. Also note that it is nearly impossible to be a victim of identity theft with this high level of monitoring.

I have never made a late payment and I pay off my credit cards in full each month. Why is my FICO credit score still so low?

An attorney friend and client of mine - let's call him John - called me, extremely frustrated. John had just been notified of his failure to qualify for a mortgage due to his low FICO score. He said, "I just don't understand. I completely pay off every credit card bill I get within a few days of receiving the statement, and I have never been late. I only have three lower-limit credit cards. I pay cash for all my cars. I thought my credit rating would be perfect. Why is my FICO score low?"

With all John's monetary assets and his obvious ability and willingness to pay his debt, the FICO computer program still saw him as a high risk for several reasons. He had too few open credit accounts and too little history. But most important, John had relatively small credit limits - a $5,000 limit on two credit cards and a $10,000 limit on a third card. John maintained these lower credit limits since he *incorrectly* assumed that lower credit limits would make him seem less risky and thus improve his FICO score. Since John entertained clients rather lavishly and often traveled internationally, it was not unusual for his credit card balances to approach their limits each month. What John did not realize was that it did not matter that he fully paid off his credit cards each month because the FICO scoring program does not consider these payments.

Thirty percent of a FICO credit score is based on "amounts owed." This roughly equates to how much of our available credit we are using. FICO scoring programs assume that if our credit cards are "maxed-out" (charges totaling close to the maximum limit) that we are getting into trouble and are a higher risk. The FICO scoring programs don't care about our payments other than if they are on time and meet the minimum payment amounts.

The credit card companies usually report to the credit agencies only once each month, and normally they report the balances shown on their monthly statements. Since John paid off his balances after he got his statements, only high balances relative to the limits were being reported. It didn't matter that he was paying off the balance each month, because the amount of the payment made is not reported to the credit reporting agencies. Since John charged up his credit cards again before the next statement, only a high balance was being reported to the credit agencies. John's large payments made no more difference to the FICO scoring program than paying the minimum since a new high balance was shown each month. The result was a low credit score for John despite excellent payment history.

I recommended two changes for John to improve his FICO score. First, he needed to ask his credit card companies to increase his credit limits. John made three quick phone calls to accomplish this. Due to his great payment history, all three credit card companies were happy to instantly double his credit limits without even checking his FICO score. (Remember, the credit card companies have our monthly payment amount history while the credit reporting agencies only have our monthly balance and minimum payment information.) This action changed his credit rating because now he was charging a lower percentage of his total allowed credit limits.

Second, John needed to change the way he made his payments. It is important that the credit cards report low monthly statement balances. Therefore, John needed to change the timing of his payments. It is possible to go online a few days before the end of each credit card's monthly cycle and make an online payment to reduce or zero out what the monthly statement balance will report. This in turn reduces what gets reported to the credit agencies. (Never make manual paper check payments to credit cards since the timing is subject to mail and other handling issues.) The timing of this is difficult since seldom will multiple credit cards' monthly cycles align with each other or with the calendar month. From a practical viewpoint, it is easier to pay off all credit cards online on the first, tenth, and twentieth of each month. This normally results in very low balances being reported to the credit agencies.

John made these two changes, and within thirty days (the time it takes for the credit card companies to automatically report limit changes and outstanding balance changes to the credit agencies), John's FICO credit score improved by 100 points. The improved FICO score dramatically affected John's business and his ability to buy the hotel he wanted to invest in.

The point of this example is that our *assumptions* about what actions positively affect our FICO scores are often incorrect. There is no substitute for learning how our FICO scores are calculated and for monitoring our FICO scores. Let's begin by learning the five categories that affect our FICO scores.

Table 13.4
Component Contributing to FICO Score***

Categories of Credit Information	Percentage of Total FICO Score
Amounts owed	30 %
New credit	10 %
Payment history	35 %
Types of credit in use	10 %
Length of credit history	15 %

***The above information was derived from www.myFICO.com on November 28, 2007.

Amounts Owed

The easiest way to improve our FICO scores is in the category of "amounts owed." We can rapidly change our score contribution from this category because it looks only at current information - balance owed, maximum credit limits, etc. Since history does not matter in this category, we can make very rapid changes to our FICO scores, like John did in the above example. Also, since this category contributes 30% to the total FICO score, the effect can be dramatic. The exact formulas for calculating FICO scores are nearly impossible to obtain. However, the basic considerations in this category are keeping each balance low relative to its maximum credit limit and keeping the total debt low relative to the combined total of all our credit cards' limits. These two considerations will help improve our FICO scores. Further, balances on only a few of our cards are far better than balances on all our cards. A tabular summary follows.

Table 13.5
How Amounts Owed Affect Our FICO Scores

Amounts Owed Issues	Affect on FICO Score
Credit card balance below 10% of card's limit	Positive
Credit card balance above 25% of card's limit	Negative
Credit card balance above 50% of card's limit	Dramatic Negative
Total owed below 10% of total of all limits	Positive
Total owed above 25% of total of all limits	Negative
Total owed above 50% of total of all limits	Dramatic Negative
Balance owed on less than 30% of cards issued to us	Positive
Balance owed on more than 50% of cards issued to us	Negative
Balance owed on all of the cards issued to us	Dramatic Negative

Minimizing the monthly reported amount owned versus our credit limit improves our FICO credit scores.

The fastest and easiest way to improve our FICO score in this area is to ask our credit card companies to increase our maximum credit limits. This normally takes only a phone call. However, when making this request, make sure to specify that this should be done without a credit inquiry. Note that credit inquiries can lower the FICO score. Just explain to the credit card customer service person that "we are applying for a new mortgage and cannot allow credit inquiries to lower our FICO score."

Generally the first credit card customer service person you speak to does not have the authority to do as you request. Do not be too shy to politely ask to speak to a manager. Often a manager will have the authority to fulfill this request. If your request is denied, the next step in playing this game is to ask to close the account. Almost always you will be switched to a special department for this request. The customer service persons in the account termination department are specially trained to "save" the account. They will ask why you wish to close the account, so you will explain that the credit limit is too low. They often have additional authority to save the account including the ability to increase credit limits. Normally they will give you what you want, and they always ask you to change your mind about closing the account. Remember, this is a head fake; you do not want to close a higher-limit credit card because it would reduce your total credit limit, which would increase your debt ratio and reduce your FICO score.

Note that not all credit card companies will allow an increase without reviewing the FICO score. You may need to allow the credit inquiry in order to increase the limits on some of the credit cards.

Some people will attempt to increase their total credit limits by opening new larger-limit credit cards. This may work well in the long run. However, this method will often result in lower FICO scores in the short run. This is because new credit cards and new credit inquiries will lower our FICO scores. If keeping a high FICO score is necessary, pursue new credit cards slowly. Open only one new card within a six-month period. Or if you know you are not going to be applying for a major loan for a year, you can apply for several cards all at once, knowing that time will reverse the drop in your FICO score over the next six to twelve months.

Some people only have one credit card. If this is true for us, any balance on that one card means that "all" our credit cards have a balance. Since all our credit cards have a balance, our FICO scores are reduced. In short, we need multiple cards. This is true for security reasons as well. If we only have one credit card on a trip and that card has a problem (lost, stolen, account issue, etc.), we could be left without a usable credit card. Credit cards can solve emergency issues. Keep several handy.

It is nearly impossible to maximize our credit scores if we make our credit card payments using paper checks and the mail system.

A maximum credit score requires low balances on credit card statements. It is impossible to achieve this goal if we wait to receive our credit card statements before we make payments. Credit card companies report to the credit agencies only once each month, and they report the balances shown on their monthly statements. We must reduce our balances before monthly statements are generated. Waiting for the monthly bill will not work. This requires an Internet connection to our accounts.

Go online three times a month, on the first, tenth, and twentieth, and review all the charges and balances. We need to review our charges and balances anyhow to prevent identity theft, monitor our spending, and verify our last payment. Making these more frequent payments will allow the monthly statement balance report to the credit agencies to show low balances.

Use each credit card's website to pay each credit card's bill. I would never recommend allowing automatic payment. This is dangerous. Only allow single, one-time-only payments to be taken from your banking account and made to the credit card account. I would *NOT* recommend using the bank's bill payment system. Instead, go on to each credit card's website and make the payment there, where it is also possible to review the details of the charges. You can't see that information on your bank's bill payment system.

For people who incorrectly believe that online payments are risky: Get over it, grandma. Mailing a paper check is far riskier for many reasons. First, many people will handle the payment envelope as it passes though the mail system and can steal our checking account information. Second, the payment-style envelope addressed to a credit card company makes it obvious that a check is enclosed and thus makes our payment an obvious target for theft. Note: Our credit card numbers are included in those envelopes. It is an unnecessary risk to send such information through the postal system. Third, the mail system is not always reliable or timely, particularly around the holiday season, versus an electronic system that provides an instant verification of delivery. A paper check in the banking system is subject to theft, handling errors, amount errors, and account assignment errors.

All the above issues are avoided when using secure electronic payments. Sure, people can do stupid things on the Internet and get defrauded. However, paying our credit card bills online is a safe and smart thing to do. Over the many years, my paper checks have gone missing, have been credited to the incorrect account, and have been credited the incorrect amount. This has never happened with an electronic payment.

New Credit

There is very little we can do to quickly improve this category. However, by doing the right things we can completely prevent this category from damaging our FICO scores within twelve months. New credit accounts and new credit inquiries occurring more frequently than once in six months will reduce our FICO scores. Simply do not apply for new credit more frequently than once in six months. Try to avoid opening accounts that are not really needed.

Minimizing the number of times we apply for new credit will improve our FICO scores.

Note that FICO scoring programs are smart enough to understand rate shopping. If there are several credit inquiries from mortgage companies or several inquires from auto finance companies within a few days, FICO assumes that rate shopping is occurring and only counts them as a single inquiry. Do not allow the time between these multiple inquiries to exceed fourteen days, or FICO may consider them as multiple inquiries and thus reduce our FICO scores.

Credit inquiries remain on our credit records for two years. However, FICO only considers the last twelve months of inquiries. Thus, within a year, any sins we have in this category are washed clean and the negative effect of newly opened accounts fades.

The important takeaway in this category is: Do not bounce around opening new accounts in order to get first-year teaser interest rates or other bonuses. Do not open a new account in order to get a free toaster. Frequent new accounts and inquiries will reduce our FICO scores. To a FICO scoring program, fast changes equate to high risk.

Payment History

This is the largest category, affecting 35% of our FICO score. It is also one of the slowest moving if we are attempting to improve our scores. Therefore, the sooner we start, the sooner we can improve our scores. This is the category in which late payments, charge-offs, collections, liens, and bankruptcies are reported. The best thing we can do is to make certain that we are never late.

Using the online, three-times-a-month, payment method will eliminate any late payments reports.

Many late payments are caused by failure to receive a statement in the mail, misplacing a statement, failure of the creditor to properly receive and record a payment, and simply forgetting to make a payment. If we use the online, three-times-a-month payment method I have suggested above, it's very unlikely that any of these mistakes will occur again. Most negative credit events remain on our records for seven years, bankruptcies for ten years. However, the negative effects of these issues reduce dramatically with time. Just make payments regularly, and the sins of the past will fade gradually. A two-year-old late payment has little effect compared to a late payment within the last three months.

How do we fix late payments and other derogatory reports? It is possible to challenge and remove negatively reported issues. If we tell a reporting agency that a derogatory report is in error, and if a creditor does not verify the derogatory report within thirty days, the reporting agency must remove the derogatory report. Occasionally this technique works, but do not count on it. Be wary of credit repair companies that promise they will use this technique to repair your credit. What fixes most FICO scores is paying on time and waiting for derogatory reports to age.

Will paying off a lien, collection account, or a charge-off improve a FICO score? Normally, only marginally, if any. The record of the derogatory report remains on our credit history for seven years even if it is paid off. I recommend negotiating with the derogatory report account, offering to pay if and only if they agree to change their reporting to "paid-as-agreed." This is the only report that does not hurt our FICO scores. If they do not agree to change their reporting, I see little reason for paying them anything. During negotiation with them, I recommend providing no personal information as they could use this for collection purposes. Remember, their negative reports will drop off our credit history seven years after it is first reported.

Types of Credit in Use
FICO programs are looking for a healthy mix of credit. What's a healthy mix? The answer is a mix that avoids extremes. For instance, the ideal number of revolving credit cards (MasterCard, Visa, American Express, etc.) is no fewer than three and no more than six. If you have fewer, consider slowly adding cards but not more than one per six months. If you have more, consider canceling some of the newer lower-limit cards.

In the seventies and eighties, many department stores and gasoline stations highly promoted their own credit cards versus MasterCard and Visa. It was not unusual to have a dozen such cards. If you still have all these cards, cancel all but a couple of the oldest of them. Keep these in order to keep an older credit history. Moving most of our charges to a couple of major credit cards will also simplify our bill paying. I know men who sit on an overly thick wallet due to a dozen gas station credit cars. Removing this lump could straighten their backs and reduce their chiropractic doctor bills.

Length of Credit History
There is very little we can do to improve this category, which accounts for about 15% of our credit score. FICO considers the oldest of our credit accounts and uses this as the age of our credit record. The older the credit record, the better our FICO score will be. We can maintain our score in this category by making sure we do not close our older accounts. Further, if we have older credit that is not showing on our credit reports, we need

to take action to ensure this favorable credit status is reported regularly. An incorrect social security number recorded by our creditor could cause this omission. Some creditors only report credit history to the credit agencies if you ask them to report.

FICO also considers the average age of our accounts. Just like in the "new credit" category, opening new accounts will shorten our average age and thus lower our scores. Conversely, closing newer accounts could lengthen our average account age and thus improve our scores.

Chapter Takeaway
FICO credit scores can dramatically affect our monthly cash flow by determining how much interest we will pay on many purchases. Negative FICO scores can prevent us from making some purchases and from being considered by some employers. It is important for us to learn how to monitor our credit reports and to learn what affects our FICO scores. Often, there are steps we can take to improve our FICO scores that in turn can change our lives.

Chapter 14
Home Sweet Mortgage

Is the place we live in a house, or is it a home? A house is a building made of brick, stone, concrete, and wood. A house is a financial asset that has taxes, insurance, and upkeep expenses along with some price appreciation potential. In contrast, a home is a feeling we have when surrounded by family and familiar items. I believe it is important to differentiate the concepts of house and home. A feeling of being home can be established even in a temporary rental apartment situation.

Decisions about houses should be based largely on financial issues such as value, affordability, tax savings, and appreciation potential. How much we can afford and how we should finance the house is a practical monetary decision. The community in which we decide to make our home is a personal and emotional decision. My point is, don't let emotions take control. Remember that housing costs are typically the largest budget expense. Buy what you need and not more.

I have seen families break down in tears as they packed up their homes and moved. It's true that packing brings back memories that can be both happy and sad. Looking at an empty house, which was once our home, can also be very sad. However, after two weeks in the new house, all the sadness is forgotten.

We discover that our memories moved with us. It is important to separate emotions about our home from the practical issue of investing in real estate through buying a personal residence. Buying a house should be primarily a monetary decision!

Is our house the best investment we will ever make? Well, hopefully not. The sad case is that a family's house is often the *only* long-term investment they make. Since many people never experience the benefits of other long-term investments, they tend to believe that their homes are and should be their biggest and best investments. They are wrong. These people, without understanding the time value of money, will offer great examples of gains without stopping to calculate and realize that the true annualized return is only marginal.

As an example, a friend of mine contends he only invests in real estate, citing a recent profit on a house. He purchased the house twenty years ago for $100,000 and just sold it for $400,000. "Wow, a $300,000 gain in twenty years!" he exclaims to me. My response is, so what! That equates to a 7.18% gain per year. That's right - if you invest $100,000 earning 7.18% over twenty years, it will become $400,000. Was the home's investment gain really only 7.18%. The answer is no! When you take out the 1% - 3% cost of property taxes each year, plus an extra 1% for property insurance each year, plus the cost of repairs and upkeep, this 7.18% gain becomes a less impressive 2% - 4% per year. Many mutual funds would have done much better, since a number of equity funds have averaged more than 11% annualized gain over the last twenty years. Investing $100,000 in a mutual fund twenty years ago averaging an 11% gain per year would have resulted in $806,231 today. Which is the better investment? Also note: The water pipes don't burst at 3:00 a.m. in a mutual fund.

Some people will say that I am ignoring the leverage factor. By this they mean that only a small down payment was used to purchase the $100,000 house in the above example. Would this make the house a better investment? My answer is no because the 6% - 8% interest paid on the mortgage and other costs would largely wipeout the 7.18% annualized gain.

Others would say that I'm ignoring the tax benefits of home ownership. It's true that the ability to deduct mortgage interest and property taxes can be a windfall for homeowners. However, some other investments (like municipal bonds) have better tax advantages. Also remember that the IRS phases out Schedule A mortgage interest deductions as our income grows. Further, property tax deductions are often eliminated by AMT (alternative minimum tax) provisions.

Our personal residences are seldom good investments when all the costs are considered. They are at best forced savings accounts paying low interest.

I don't mean to discourage people from buying a home. I believe that home ownership often makes more financial sense than renting. Whether buying or renting a house, the transaction is an expense and *not an investment*. Try to minimize that expense. Real estate is an investment only if it is producing income. I would not characterize a personal residence as an investment. However, I certainly would classify income-producing rental property as an investment. If we could choose between buying a large house for our personal residence or buying two smaller houses, one for ourselves and the other as a rental property, I would recommend the second option.

Many newlyweds get this bad advice from parents and friends: "Buy the biggest house you can as soon as you can." Why do people give this bad advice? It is because their houses are the only long-term investments they have been able to attain and hold on to. Thus, they mistakenly believe a house is a good investment. When they've only held one long-term investment, obviously that investment looks good.

Again, our houses are forced savings accounts. I recommend more discipline in our finances, thus providing enough funds to make other investments that far outperform housing. If the people making the above recommendation had the discipline, they would have experienced other long-term investments and would recommend more than just personal houses.

On a long-term basis, house prices cannot appreciate more than people's ability to afford them; therefore, long-term price appreciation is limited to the rate of wage inflation.

Is a house a good investment? First, let's define a good investment as one that increases in value faster than the inflation rate. Therefore, buying a house to speculate on its appreciation is a bad investment. This is because house prices are limited to people's ability to afford them. Over the long run, house prices cannot grow faster than wage inflation. Since house prices cannot increase faster than the wage inflation rate, they are bad investments.

Certain social changes have temporarily modified the above relationship. In the 1960s, most families had one wage earner, and only about 25% of the family's income was dedicated to housing. Over the next forty years, the increasing trend towards families with two wage earners made it possible to dedicate 35% to 40% of the family's income to housing. This trend allowed for prices to temporarily rise faster than wage inflation and remain affordable. However, I believe it's unlikely that a larger percentage of the family budget could go towards housing. Therefore, I believe that further housing appreciation is limited to wage inflation.

House prices do not only move due to wage inflation. Affordability is another factor, and it is mostly driven by mortgage interest rates. Lower rates equate to higher house prices, and higher rates equate to lower house prices. If mortgage rates are high and likely to come down, then it is also likely that house prices will rise as rates decrease. The opposite is also true.

House prices often move in short spurts with long periods of flat or declining prices between the bursts. Therefore, the best time to buy is after a long period of flat or declining prices when mortgage interest rates are above their historical norms. The last time we saw these conditions on the national level was in 1998. Wow, what a time to buy! However, that gravy train ended in most U.S. markets during the summer of 2005. John Talbott successfully predicted this decline in the book *The Coming Crash in the Housing Market*. I highly recommend reading this book, even though its 2003 printing date is a little old. This book explains the price movement of housing and thus gives the reader good knowledge on when to buy real estate.

My point is, do not expect real estate values to always increase. There have been and will continue to be periods of time in which real estate values decline. From a long-term perspective, the gains we have seen in the last forty years are above normal. Long-term housing prices rise with wage inflation. Housing cost is an expense, not an investment; - try to minimize that expense. Housing is an investment only if it is income-producing rental property.

Why is rental property an investment when our personal homes are not? There is a significant difference. With rental property, two things are increasing with the rate of wage inflation: both the value of the property and the rents collected. Thus, long-term growth at twice the rate of wage inflation is possible; this is a significant difference. The ability to depreciate rental property is an additional tax benefit.

Mortgage Rates

How do we minimize our mortgage expense? The best answer is to never quit shopping for better interest rates. Shop as many sources as possible before selecting a mortgage company. Then once they have closed the mortgage, continue to shop. If we could get our bosses to give us a pay raise just by asking for it, would we ask? Reducing our mortgage payment is effectively the same as a pay raise and may be much easier to obtain. Continue asking the current mortgage company and other companies if they can provide better interest rates.

Even if the markets do not provide lower interest rates, we may be able to get a lower interest rate by improving our credit scores (see chapter 13). After improving our FICO credit scores, it is time to write our own raise by refinancing the house and reducing our mortgage payments.

Where do we shop for lower rates? It is easy to check the prevailing mortgage interest rates online - just Google "mortgage rates." Sites such as www.myFICO.com have rate quotes. Ask a loan broker to place you on their rate alert e-mail list.

When should we check mortgage rates? Two days after the Federal Reserve has taken action or anytime our FICO credit score improves are both good times. At a minimum, I believe we should check every six weeks. If the rates are getting close to where we should refinance, then check more often. When rates approach our desired target, it is time to contact a lender or mortgage broker.

When shopping for mortgage rates, be careful not to damage our FICO credit score. Remember that frequent credit inquiries will lower our FICO scores. If we ask someone to check out loan rates, remind them that we are not authorizing them to pull a credit report. If they insist that checking our credit will not hurt our FICO scores, we are talking to a liar, so just move on to the next lender. We should provide the lender with our FICO scores, which we should know and monitor from subscribing to Score Watch on www.myFICO.com (see chapter 13). If the lender asks for a social security number, just say no. They want this because they intend to pull a credit report on us. We should tell them that we are not applying at this point and will not apply until we have a preliminary interest rate quote. Provide them with your FICO score and no more. If they insist on a social security number, just move to the next lender. Remember, it's possible that they are attempting to steal your identity - be judicial when revealing social security numbers.

Shop for the lowest APR interest rate, not the lowest payment amount.

Shop for the government-regulated APR interest rate, not just for the lowest payments. The lenders can manipulate payments and other interest rate quotes. Low teaser rates have fooled many homeowners, who were surprised to discover much higher payments later. Watch out for option ARMs and other exotic mortgage products that may have lower payments but also may have negative amortization - the balance owed goes up every month instead of down. Avoid predator mortgage products that are looking to attract us with short-term benefits and then slaughter us with the small print. Remember, the devil is in the details, and not many of us can understand all the detailed small print. Stick with well-known major lenders.

Figures don't lie, but liars figure. Along with many good people, many unscrupulous lenders and mortgage brokers can be found in the mortgage industry. Generally, don't respond to mail, phone, and Internet advertising to refinance the house. It is from these lenders that most of the unscrupulous loans are originated. Never give out personal information to a cold caller. Never give out personal information unless you initiated the contact.

I have received several telephone solicitations from people claiming to be with my current mortgage lender who in fact were not affiliated. Remember that basic information about our current mortgage (original amount and who financed with) is public information that unscrupulous people will obtain and use to solicit additional information from us. Do we want someone we don't know to have access to all our personal financial information to qualify us for a loan? Could they be out to steal our identities and credit card information? Again, never give out personal information unless you initiated the contact.

It is often much better to go with a lender or broker with whom we are familiar. It's best to work with a lender or mortgage broker who cares what we think about him next year! It's not likely that they will put us in a predatory mortgage product.

Closing Cost

We must make sure that we are comparing apples with apples and not with oranges. If we are shopping for a thirty-year fixed mortgage with no points or closing costs, make sure everyone is quoting the same product. If someone is quoting an interest-only loan or a loan with two points, their quotes could be quite different and misleading. When we cannot get exactly the same product quotes from various loan companies, the government-regulated APR (annual percentage rate) can sometimes help. The calculation of this APR number takes into effect some of the cost and tries to level the field among various products. The APR number is far from perfect, but it may help. As an example, today's www.Ditect.com website is quoting a thirty-year fixed rate of 4.625% with two points. The government requires them to quote an APR of 4.929%. If we refuse to pay the discount points, our true interest rate would be closer to the APR percentage.

What are points, and why do I need to pay them?

Points are percentage points of the loan amount. One point on a $150,000 loan would be $1,500. Two points would be $3,000. One and a half points on a $300,000 loan would be $4,500. Points are used to pay two expenses: loan origination cost (including commissions) and loan discount buy downs.

The cost for originating a loan will vary between $2,000 and $3,500 depending on the lending institution. This cost is relatively fixed regardless of the size of the loan. If we are asked to pay both a loan origination fee and separate points, it is likely that the points are profit going to the loan broker. Try to negotiate down both the origination fee and the points. If we are financing less than $200,000, we can expect to pay a loan origination fee or points equal to the fixed origination cost. As loan amounts become higher, they become more profitable, and mortgage companies can afford to pay more of the origination cost themselves. The larger the loan, the more successful our negotiation will be. As loan amounts increase, lenders are able to absorb the entire loan origination cost, and we can expect to get no-cost loans. Depending on the institution, loan amounts somewhere between $400,000 and $700,000 will justify a no-cost loan.

Discount points are paid to lower the interest cost. We may "buy down" our mortgage interest rate by paying points. This amounts to "prepaid" interest. In fact, the IRS requires us to amortize this cost as interest expense over the life of the loan. In short, discount points are a scheme to make us incorrectly believe we are getting a lower interest rate. Paying discount points may actually cost us more in the long run, particularly if we sell or refinance in the near future. Never pay discount points. However, when buying a house, it is always okay to ask the seller to pay discount points for us, so we'll get a lower interest rate at the seller's expense.

The important thing to remember is that some lenders' charges are negotiable. Try to lower the refinancing cost. Lenders will almost always offer to roll the origination cost into the new loan, thus increasing our loan balance. The fact that they will add their charges to our loan should not sway us. They will argue how little this additional debt increases our payment. Just say no. Paying their fees over thirty years with interest is no deal. Negotiate their charges as low as possible. The most effective way to do this is to use one lender's quote against the other to get them to move lower on their lender charges.

Understand that there can often be six hands between us and the firm actually making the mortgage loan. All these hands are trying to take a small fee off the top. Many may be willing to take less just to get the deal to go through. Don't be shy about asking them to take less. Or find another lender with fewer hands involved.

Types of Mortgages

Are interest-only loans a good idea? To understand this issue, we must first understand how loans work. With a thirty-year 6% fixed-rate mortgage, only about 14.2% of the first year's payments reduce principal. That means that 85.8% of our monthly payments are characterized as interest payments. Many institutions allow interest-only loans that reduce our payments by that 14.2%. With these loans, our payments will not reduce the balance owed. Although I like paying down the balance, selecting an interest-only loan is a reasonable way to reduce our payments. These loans are far better than some teaser rate loans. Taking out a five-, seven-, or ten-year interest-only loan has far less risk than using a one-year ARM (Adjustable Rate Mortgage) to reduce payments.

What term of mortgage loan should we consider? Are five- or seven-year ARMs too risky? The first thing we need to consider is how long we plan to own the house. If we are young and upwardly mobile, are we therefore likely to be moving to a bigger house? Are we in a profession that requires a lot of moving? Are we mid-career stable and unlikely to move? Are we nearing retirement and likely to move to our beach retirement house soon? The point is that homeownership duration is a very personal issue. Keep in mind that the average length of homeownership is about seven years.

For this reason, I believe that five- and seven-year ARMs are reasonable alternatives for many homebuyers. Unlike one-year ARMs, which reset their interest rates every year, these loans have steady payments for five or seven years. These loans may have a ¾ percentage point lower interest rate than a thirty-year fixed loan and are thus affordable. During this five- to seven-year period, we can be looking for opportunities to refinance with another ARM and thus restart the five- to seven-year period. This is highly likely to occur since most interest rate cycles are less than seven years in duration. During the five- to seven-year period, we will probably sell our homes anyway.

Meanwhile, lower mortgage payments will help us put more money into our freedom accounts.

One-year ARMs provide the lowest interest rates. However, I advise against these loans unless there is certainty the house will sell within a year. One-year ARMs are useful for house flippers - people who buy, refurbish, and quickly resell. One-year ARMs are too risky for most people. If we can't afford a thirty-year fixed loan, we shouldn't use an ARM to force our way in; doing so is economic suicide. Not being able to qualify for the thirty-year fixed loan payment is a clue that the house is too expensive for us. If we are depending on the house value to increase or our incomes to increase, neither will happen. The economic "I told you so" gods will slap us down while laughing at us for being so stupid. The only economic plans that work are the ones that allow for unexpected things to happen.

Thirty-year fixed loans are ideal for people staying put. However, never say "never." It is impossible to predict the future as unforeseen events often change our life plans. If rates are historically low or if there is little interest savings with an ARM product, by all means choose a fifteen-, twenty-, or thirty-year fixed loan. Never go with an ARM if it only offers a marginal interest savings. For rental property, I prefer twenty-year fixed loans.

Some people prefer the lower payments of a thirty-year loan but also desire the earlier payoff. An alternative to a fifteen- or twenty-year term loan is a thirty-year loan, but with making additional payments, such as making thirteen or fourteen payments instead of the normal twelve payments per year.

If the mortgage allows for additional early principal payments, this can substantially reduce both the mortgage length and the total interest paid over the life of the mortgage. This works when the principal from which the interest payment is being calculated is being reduced by these extra payments. This allows more of each future payment to pay down more principal instead of interest. However, some mortgages only allocate extra payments to remove payments from the end of the loan. If this is the case, put the extra payments in a separate interest-bearing account.

Another early payoff technique is to make mortgage payments every other week. This program fits some people's biweekly paycheck budget better. The twenty-six biweekly payments equate to thirteen monthly payments per year and thus pays off the mortgage quicker. Some lenders allow borrowers to convert existing loans to such a program, while other lenders can automatically adjust for our more frequent payments. A rental property owner may want to make larger payments every month that the property is fully occupied and reduce this payment to the normal payment when vacancies occur.

As we have discussed, we want to remain flexible and able to take advantage of market conditions by refinancing. Therefore, we should obtain loans that have no prepayment penalty. Some loans require prepayment penalties if we sell or refinance our houses within the first one to three years. Since we never know what the future will bring, try to avoid these loans. Don't forget to ask about prepayment penalties when getting a new loan.

Using Loan Brokers Versus Dealing Directly with Lenders

Should we use an independent loan broker or deal directly with a lending institution? The answer depends a lot on our personal situations. If we have a complicated financial picture or a lower FICO credit score, brokers may be our best answer because they can "shop" the loan around to many lenders. A broker may also simplify the information collection process. However, in some circumstances, the use of a broker can add to the closing costs. After all, the broker is an additional hand between us and the money. If we have a good credit score and a simple W2 income source, working directly with lenders may be the best choice.

Private Mortgage Insurance (PMI)

When borrowers make only a small down payment, less than 20%, most private lenders protect themselves by requiring us to purchase PMI. If we have a government-insured FHA (Federal Housing Administration) or VA (Veterans Administration) loan, we are exempt from the PMI requirement. FHA and VA loans have loan amount limits that make them unavailable in higher-priced markets like New York or California. For higher-priced homes, PMI is an expensive add-on to our monthly payments that should be avoided.

The economic relief act of 2008 temporarily increased the FHA loan limits dramatically to $729,750. FHA loans allow only a 5% down payment without PMI. With this new law, we may be able to refinance under the new guidelines and avoid PMI. Check with your lender.

How much is PMI? PMI costs vary but average about 0.52%. Thus the PMI cost on a $200,000 loan would be about $1,000 per year or $83 per month. The PMI cost on a $500,000 loan would be about $2,500 per year or $208 per month. The above assumes a 10% down payment was made. With only a 5% down payment, PMI rates increase to 0.78%.

How can we avoid PMI if we only have a 10% down payment? The answer is an 80-10-10 loan. Instead of a first mortgage loan for 90% of the purchase price and a 10% down payment, we obtain an 80% first mortgage loan plus a second loan for 10% of the purchase price, followed with a 10% down payment. This 80% first mortgage loan will not require PMI and may be at a lower rate since only 80% is being borrowed. The 10% second mortgage will have a higher interest rate, maybe 2% more. However, this 2% more is only on the second mortgage, which is only 10% of the total purchase cost. 2% more on the 10% is far less than paying 0.52% on 90%. Thus, the additional interest cost of the second loan may be far less than the cost of PMI.

I am always amazed at loan brokers who do not recommend the 80-10-10 solution to their clients who have low down payments. Back away from brokers who do not examine the alternatives to paying PMI. We don't want brokers who don't have our best interests at heart.

If we are currently paying PMI, how do we cancel this insurance? When our home equity reaches 20% of the home's value, we are entitled to cancel PMI. Our equity increases as our loan balance decreases or as our home value increases. Market movements and home improvements can justify the price increases. For loans originated after July 30, 1999, the lender is required to tell us when we can cancel PMI. However, don't hold your breath waiting for this notice. If you think your home equity exceeds 20%, call the mortgage company and request cancellation of PMI. This may require hiring an appraiser. Also note that this cannot be done in the first two years of a loan. During this period, only refinancing without PMI can remove this expense.

Eliminating PMI is another justification of refinancing. It may be well worth it to refinance at the same mortgage interest rate if we are eliminating the extra 0.52% charge that PMI is costing.

Conforming Versus Jumbo Loans
Conforming loans have terms and conditions that follow the guidelines set forth by Fannie Mae and Freddie Mac. These government sponsored companies purchase mortgage loans that comply with their guidelines from mortgage lenders. Loans that comply with these guidelines typically have much lower interest rates. The key conforming issue is loan size. At the beginning of 2008, the conforming loan limits for single-family homes was $417,000. However, an economic incentive package of 2008 temporarily increased this limit to $729,750.

Loan amounts higher than the limit are considered jumbo loans that normally carry a significantly higher interest rate. As of this writing, jumbo loans carry an interest rate that is 1.0 to 1.25% higher than conforming loans. Converting from a jumbo loan to a conforming loan is a huge refinancing opportunity.

A recent ¾ point reduction in the federal funds rate only resulted in a $1/8$ point mortgage interest rate reduction. In contrast, this rule change could bring a huge transformation in the affordability of our houses. If our current mortgage is a jumbo loan, check if significant savings can be captured by refinancing to a conforming loan instead.

If the loan amount is just above the new conforming loan limits, it may still make economic sense to use a conforming loan for the maximum amount allowed coupled with a second mortgage for the remaining required loan amount. This is similar to the 80-10-10 strategy I recommended to avoid PMI. The second mortgage will have a higher interest rate. However, if the balance borrowed on the second loan is relatively small, the effective blended interest rate of the conforming first loan and the small second loan could be far lower than a nonconforming jumbo loan interest rate on the entire loan balance.

Chapter Takeaway

Housing cost is typically the largest part of our budgets. By gaining control of our housing expense, we allow ourselves to invest in other areas that are typically far more profitable. Don't consider your personal residence as an investment. It's not. Don't buy a too large or too expensive home. Don't consider our housing cost as fixed. Make appropriate changes to economize on housing cost. Many of these changes may not require moving. Some of the ways we can reduce the cost of our current houses include:

1) Shop for better interest rates and refinance.
2) Improve our FICO credit scores so we can get better mortgage rates.
3) Check if the new conforming and FHA maximums allow us to get better rates.
4) Take steps to eliminate PMI cost.
5) Don't buy a home that is too expensive

Chapter 15
The Power of Compounding
(Are We Getting Ahead?)

Before we begin discussing types of investments, we must understand the importance of the time value of money. Stated another way, we must understand the advantage of compounding investment gains. Specifically, we need to understand how a small change in investment return expectations can result in a significant difference over a long period of time.

How significant is this difference? Will doubling our investment gains from 5% to 10% also double the money we have in many years? The answer is no - the effect is larger! A doubling in annual investment gains with compounding will result in far more than doubling our money over a long period of time. A $10,000 investment with a 5% compounding gain over thirty years results in a nest egg of $43,219. However, a $10,000 investment with a 10% (double the 5% gain) compounding gain over thirty years results in a nest egg of $174,494. Thus the return from an investment yielding 10% is four times larger than an investment yielding 5% over thirty years. Wow, what a difference!

But this difference is not linear. If we double our investment gain again from 10% to 20%, the compounding effect is much larger. A $10,000 investment with a 20% compounding gain over thirty years results in a nest egg of $2,373,763. This is 13.6 times larger than the $174,494 results of a 10% investment return over the same period. Even more staggering is that this $2,373,763 nest egg is 54.9 times larger that the $43,219 results of a 5% investment return over the same thirty-year period. This is possible because of the magic of compounding returns.

The concept and benefits of compounding returns needs to be fully understood!

What does compounding mean? It means that not only do we make gains off our initial investments, but also that in subsequent periods we make gains off accumulated gains from previous periods. In summary, our babies have their own babies.

Let's explain this with an example where we invest $1,000 and have investment gains of 10% per year. Without compounding, a 10% gain on $1,000 would yield $100 per year. At the end of four years, without compounding, we would simply add each year's gain and have a total of $1,400.

With compounding, we would have a balance of $1,100 at the end of the first year. During the second year, we would receive a 10% return on the beginning balance of $1,100, resulting in a $110 gain. The second year would end with $1,210. In the third year, we would earn 10% of $1,210, or $121. The third year would end with $1,331 in our coffers. In the fourth year, we would earn 10% of $1,331, or $133. The fourth year would end with $1,464 in our coffers. This compounding results in $1,464 versus the non-compounding result of $1,400. The effect of compounding dramatically grows with increasing rates and with increasing time.

The rule of 72 gives us a simple tool to estimate the time required to double our money.

There is a simple tool to estimate the effect of compounding: it's called the rule of 72. This rule allows us to estimate the period of time it takes to double our money with a given investment return rate. The rule states that by dividing 72 by our assumed investment return rate we will approximate the number of years it takes to double our money.

For a 5% return, the rule estimates that we will double our money in 14.4 years (72 / 5). How many times will we double our money in 30 years? The answer is 30 years divided by the 14.4 doubling period, or 2.0833 times (30 / 14.4). So how much will $10,000 grow in 30 years at 5%? This answer is $10,000 doubled once is $20,000, doubled again is $40,000. Now, how do we estimate the remaining fractional 0.0833 doubling? We should add 1 to the fractional remaining doubling number to get 1.0833 and then multiply this number with the last "whole number double": $40,000. This gives a result of $43,332. This estimate is very close to the correct amount of $43,219.

Table 15.1

Growth of $10,000 at Various Interest Rates of Various Periods

Interest Rates	10 Years	15 Years	20 Years	25 Years	30 Years	35 Years
2.0	$12,190	$13,459	$12,682	$16,406	$18,114	$19,999
3.0	$13,439	$15,580	$14,258	$20,938	$24,273	$28,139
4.0	$14,802	$18,009	$16,010	$26,658	$32,434	$39,461
5.0	$16,289	$20,789	$17,959	$33,864	$43,219	$55,160
7.5	$20,610	$29,589	$23,818	$60,983	$87,550	$125,689
10.0	$25,937	$41,772	$31,384	$108,347	$174,494	$281,024
12.5	$32,473	$58,518	$41,099	$190,026	$342,433	$617,075
15.0	$40,456	$81,371	$53,503	$329,190	$662,118	$1,331,755
17.5	$50,162	$112,349	$69,256	$563,568	$1,262,223	$2,826,997
20.0	$61,917	$154,070	$89,161	$953,962	$2,373,763	$5,906,682
22.5	$76,096	$209,914	$114,191	$1,597,358	$4,406,387	$12,155,228
25.0	$93,132	$284,217	$145,519	$2,646,978	$8,077,936	$24,651,903
27.5	$113,528	$382,519	$184,553	$4,342,648	$14,632,062	$49,301,084
30.0	$137,858	$511,859	$232,981	$7,056,410	$26,199,956	$97,278,604

Let's test this rule of 72 again by determining how much $10,000 will grow in 30 years at 10%. We must first determine the doubling period by dividing 72 by 10. This implies that it takes 7.2 years to double at this 10% rate. In 30 years we will double our money 4.1667 times (30 / 7.2). We obtain our answer by doubling $10,000 once to get $20,000, doubling the second time to get $40,000, doubling the third time to get $80,000, and then doubling the fourth time to get $160,000. We should add 1 to the fractional remaining doubling number to get 1.1667 and then multiply this number with the last whole number double: $160,000. This gives a result of $186,672. This estimate is close to the correct amount of $174,494.

As the investment return rate increases, the rule of 72 becomes less accurate. However, having a tool to estimate how quickly our money will double is useful. There is a compound investment return tool available at www.poor-no-more.com that will provide a more accurate result. Or, you can peruse the table below to see the effect of various investment return rates over various time horizons.

The Tax Man Cometh (After Tax Rate of Return)

Before we look at the above table and celebrate how rich our investments are going to make us, there are a couple of reality checks we need to consider. The first is how taxes will affect our wealth.

When projecting our future wealth, we must consider the effect of taxes reducing our wealth. When we first start acquiring wealth, the taxes on our investment income will hardly be noticed. However, as our nest eggs or freedom accounts grow, these taxes become huge and could significantly affect the growth of our freedom accounts.

We need to deduct the effect of taxes from our stated investment gain before we plug this number into the above table or the rule of 72 calculations. As an example, if our before-tax investment gain is 10% and our tax rate is 30%, our after-tax effective investment return is 7%. That is calculated as follows:

After-tax gain = total gain x (1 - (tax rate / 100))
After-tax gain = 10% x (1 - (30% / 100))
After-tax gain = 10% x (0.70)
After-tax gain = 7%

This 7% number and not the 10% number should be plugged into the above table or used in the rule of 72 calculations to determine our future wealth.

We cannot just look at our tax return or paycheck stub and determine our tax rate. First, we must understand how various types of investments and investment accounts are taxed quite differently. Below is an abbreviated list:

1) Tax-free municipal bond income
2) Tax-deferred retirement account income - IRA, SEP-IRA, 401(k), 403(b), and pensions
3) Tax-advantaged accounts - annuities
4) Tax-free accounts - Roth IRAs
5) Qualifying dividends
6) Long-term capital gains
7) Short-term capital gains
8) Ordinary dividends and interest income
9) The effect of state taxes

Municipal bond income is tax-free at the federal level - IRS. This is true if we own a municipal bond directly or indirectly through a mutual fund or unit trust. Municipal bonds are taxed on state tax returns unless the bond is issued in the state in which we live. In this case, we call the bonds double tax-free.

All investments in retirement accounts, IRA, SEP IRA, 401(k), 403(b), and pension plans grow tax-*deferred* regardless of the type of income these investments generate. In fact, we normally get a current year tax deduction for placing money into these accounts. The retirement account "wrapper" protects the contents of these accounts from taxation until we withdraw the money. Withdrawals from these accounts are at the highest tax rate: ordinary income rate. Unlike the annuities below, every dollar we remove from these accounts is fully taxed. Withdrawals can also be penalized an extra 10% if withdrawn before age fifty-nine and a half. If we are going to purchase an investment that generates high ordinary income or short-term capital gains, it's best to place these investments in an IRA since they will not be taxed until we make withdrawals.

All investments in annuities grow tax-*deferred*. However, we do *not* get a current year tax deduction for placing money into annuities. There are no taxes on the withdrawal of principal contribution into annuities. Withdrawals of gains from annuities are at the highest tax rate: ordinary income rate. The catch: the IRS requires us to withdraw and pay taxes on all gains before we can withdraw our principal contribution tax-free. Annuitization can avoid some of this tax issue. Withdrawals can also be penalized an extra 10% if taken before age fifty-nine and a half.

All investments in Roth IRAs grow *tax-free*. Withdrawals of principal contribution or gains from Roth IRAs are not taxed if over age fifty-nine and a half and if they have been in the Roth for five years. However, we do *not* get a current year tax deduction for placing money into Roth IRAs.

Many domestic stocks pay "qualifying dividends" that are taxed at the lower capital gains tax rate. This rate is capped at 15%. This is much less than the ordinary rate, which could be as high as 35%.

When an investment is sold, a capital gains tax is due on any profit. The profit is the difference between the sales proceeds and the total purchase cost. Investments held longer than twelve months qualify for long-term capital gains rate. This rate is capped at 15% - much lower than the maximum ordinary rate of 35%.

When an investment is sold within twelve months of the purchase, the profit is considered a short-term capital gain subject to ordinary tax rates.

Non-qualifying or ordinary dividends and interest income is taxed at ordinary tax rates.

Most states also charge taxes on investment income and gains. However, the states of Alaska, Florida, Nevada, South Dakota, Texas, Washington, and Wyoming are exceptions. The states of New Hampshire and Tennessee only tax dividends and interest but not other income. The remaining states do not make a distinction between ordinary income and long-term capital gains. These states have the same tax rates on all classes of income.

The next issue we need to determine is our *marginal* ordinary tax rate. Looking at our tax returns or at our paychecks for this information will only yield our average tax rate. We need to know our marginal tax rate. Why? Because one additional dollar of investment income will not be taxed at our average tax rate: it will be taxed at our marginal rate. This can best be determined by examining table 15.2 below.

Table 15.2
Year 2008 Marginal Federal Tax Rates

Marginal Tax Rate	Single	Head of Household	Married Filing Separately	Married Filing Jointly
10%	$0 – $8,025	$0 – $11,450	$0 – $8,025	$0 – $16,050
15%	$8,025 – $32,550	$11,450 – $43,650	$8,025 – $32,550	$16,050 – $65,100
25%	$32,550 – $78,850	$43,650 – $112,650	$32,550 – $65,725	$65,100 – $131,450
28%	$78,850 – $164,550	$112,650 – $182,400	$65,725 – $100,150	$131,450 – $200,300
33%	$164,550 – $357,700	$182,400 – $357,700	$100,150 – $178,850	$200,300 – $357,700
35%	Over $357,700	Over $357,700	Over $178,850	Over $357,700

Before using this table, we should first reduce our income by our personal exemptions plus either our standard deduction or itemized deductions. Personal exemptions for 2008 are valued at $3,500 for ourselves, our spouses, and for each of our children. The standard deduction for year 2008 is shown in table 15.3 below. If we choose to itemize deductions (instead of using the standard deduction), these deductions would include state income taxes paid, property taxes paid, and mortgage interest paid.

Table 15.3

2008 Standard Deductions

Single	Head of Household	Married Filing Separately	Married Filing Jointly
$5,450	$8,000	$5,450	$10,900

The above marginal tax rates apply to ordinary job-related income, withdrawals from retirement accounts (other than a Roth IRA), withdrawals of gains from annuities, short-term capital gains (less than twelve months), interest income, and non-qualifying dividends.

Qualifying dividends and long-term capital gains are taxed at the lower capital gains rate, which is only 5% if we are in the 10% or 15% marginal tax bracket (see table 15.2). If we are in the 25% or above marginal tax bracket, our long-term capital gains tax is capped at 15%.

We should reduce our anticipated investment returns by the marginal tax rate calculated above before we plug these numbers into table 15.1 to calculate our long-term wealth prospects.

"Real" After-Tax Rate of Return

The second issue reducing our future wealth is inflation. The effect of inflation is compounded over time and reduces the value of our money in the future. Thus, table 15.1 has little value unless we also consider the effect of inflation. Yes, $10,000 growing at 5% will grow to $43,219 in thirty years, but what will $43,219 be worth in thirty years?

"Real" rate of return is defined as our effective rate of return after the effects of inflation are considered. "Real after-tax rate of return" refers to the investment returns that include the effects of both taxes and inflation.

A common mistake is to simply subtract the assumed inflation rate from the investment return rate to yield a "real" rate of return. Like the rule of 72, this method can provide an approximation, but results in significant errors if the time period is long and interest rate is high. A calculation is available at www.poor-no-more.com to help readers get a more accurate analysis of compounding real after-tax rate of return.

Going back to my previous question, $10,000 growing at 5% will grow to $43,219 in thirty years, but what will $43,219 be worth in thirty years? Let's assume we have an inflation rate of 3%. If we simply subtract the 3% inflation rate from our 5% return rate, our "real" return rate would be 2% (5% - 3% = 2%). Now, going to table 15.1 and growing $10,000 at 2% over thirty years results in a nest egg of $19,999.

What does this mean? First understand that our $10,000 will actually grow to $43,219. However, it will only be worth

$19,999 in today's dollars. What does "in today's dollars" mean? It means that the $43,219 will buy the same stuff in thirty years that $19,999 will buy today. By subtracting an assumed inflation rate from our investment return, we can approximate the "real" future value "in today's dollars."

Now let's put this all together. Let's examine an investment that yields 10% per year in ordinary interest income. Let's assume we are in a 25% marginal tax bracket and that inflation will be steady at 2.5% per year. What will our $10,000 nest egg grow to in thirty years?

First let's consider the effect of taxes using the equation shown earlier in this chapter:

After-tax gain = total gain x (1 - (tax rate / 100))

After-tax gain = 10% x (1 − (25% / 100))

After-tax gain = 10% x (0.75)

After-tax gain = 7.5%

Using table 15.1 we see that our $10,000 will grow to an $87,550 nest egg with the 7.5% after-tax investment return. But with inflation, what will this nest egg equate to in today's dollars? This can be approximated by subtracting the inflation rate assumption, 2.5%, from the after-tax rate of return, 7.5%, to obtain the real after-tax rate of return, 7.5% - 2.5% = 5%. Now using this real after-tax rate of return, we can calculate our nest egg in today's dollars. Using a 5% return in table 15.1

yields a $43,219 nest egg. This is what the $87,555 nest egg will spend like in thirty years in today's dollars. Again it is much easier to download the real after-tax compound Excel spreadsheet from www.poor-no-more.com and let the computer make these calculations.

Chapter Takeaway

In summary, it is important to have a basic understanding of how money grows through compounding investment returns. From that, we can understand that increasing our investment returns from 5% to 10% will not just result in a simple doubling of our money available. Over thirty years the difference in our available money is quadrupled. If we increase our investment returns from 5% to 20% our available money will be 54.9 times larger in thirty years. It is also important to understand how investment returns are taxed and how inflation affects their growth.

Chapter 16
Investments Aren't Mysterious

Let's see if we can simplify what many books overcomplicate: investing. Most everything we can use as an investment vehicle can be put into one of four different "buckets." These buckets are: stocks, bonds, prepackaged managed investments, and alternative investments. Let's define them.

Stocks: A stock is a piece of a company. If we buy a share of stock, we become shareholders, or co-owners, in the company.

Bonds: If we buy a bond, we are essentially loaning money to someone, and that someone promises to pay us a regular interest payment for a set period of time, after which point we are supposed to get our money back in full.

Prepackaged Managed Investments: This includes mutual funds, ETFs, ETNs, and unit trusts.

Alternative Investments: This is a big bucket that encompasses an array of investments. Let's imagine that this bucket has four compartments, which are real estate (yes, we can invest in real estate without getting a mortgage loan!), hedge funds, private equity, and commodities and futures. These will be explained shortly.

Stocks

One day in kindergarten, my pal Billy asked if I would "share" my cupcake with him. Already an entrepreneur, I said no, but I gladly offered to sell him half of my cupcake for a nickel. As I pocketed my just-earned nickel, the chubby kid Tommy walked by and offered Billy a dime for his "share." Billy traded his "share" and doubled his nickel within seconds. We had all experienced our first "share exchange"! I got a nickel from the original trade, and Billy got a nickel of gain from his transaction with Tommy. Note, I didn't profit from the exchange between Billy and Tommy.

Companies do this same thing. They sell shares of their companies in order to raise money for ongoing operations. When a company first offers its shares to the public, we call it an Initial Public Offering, or IPO. Like my cupcake sale, companies receive funds only from the original sale of their shares to investors. Companies do not participate in the subsequent sales in the open market, that is, the stock exchange, much like how I didn't get anything from the transaction between Billy and Tommy.

When we purchase stock, we become shareholders, or co-owners, of the company. If management of a company divides the ownership of the company into 100 shares and we buy one share, then we own 1% of the company. More realistically, a company would issue 100 million shares. If we buy 100 shares, we will own 0.0001% of the company. As shareholders and co-owners, we expect to participate in the company's earnings or to receive dividends; we also expect the company to grow and thus the value of our shares to increase.

Many years ago, entrepreneurial people who traded shares of stock started congregating under a shade tree in New York City. Well, the New York Stock Exchange has grown a little since then. But people there are still doing the same thing: trading shares, hoping for them to appreciate while paying dividends.

What is the value of our shares? As they represent a fractional ownership in the company, their value will depend on the total value of the company. The value of the company mainly depends on its current profit and future profit expectations (and thus current and future profits of each share).

Let's imagine we own a house for rent. What is the value of the house? Well, that depends on how much rental income we can reasonably anticipate to collect. The rental money we collect would be our revenue. But the revenue does not equal the profit. The profit is what is left after paying the expenses related to owning and maintaining the house: property taxes, mortgage interest, repairs, and management – you get the point. In the corporate world, this remaining profit is called earnings. The total earnings divided by the number of shares gives us *earnings per share*, a very important measure for valuing shares of stock.

The most common tool to measure the value of a company's stock is its *price/earnings (P/E) ratio*. This ratio is calculated by dividing the current stock price by the company's earnings per share. For example, if a company's earnings are $10 per share and its stock is trading at $100 per share, the company's P/E ratio will be $100 / $10 = 10. Thus companies with high earnings trading at low share prices have low P/E ratios. This is not necessarily good or bad by itself. Generally, a low P/E ratio indicates that the stock is being sold at a better value: we are getting a better deal. This is like buying a share of the cupcake for a nickel instead of a dime. However, a high P/E can be justified if the company's revenues and earnings are growing rapidly. Isn't this what we want? Keep in mind that past earnings and growth do affect the price of a stock. However, the future anticipated growth and earnings will generally have a larger effect on the stock's price. The dividends that stocks pay will also affect the stocks' prices.

Bonds

A bond is essentially a loan. My "never can get it right" brother-in-law keeps asking to borrow money so that he can start his next hair-brained get-rich-quick business venture. He tells me not to worry because he's giving me his "bond" that he will pay me back. He is also promising to pay me interest quarterly with a lump sum repayment in full in ten years. My loan to my brother-in-law would be similar to an unrated unsecured corporate bond.

When we buy a bond, we basically loan an entity a portion of the funds they need. This entity can be a corporation, government, or bank. When lending money, we want to know the maturity (when our money will be returned to us), the interest rate, and the credit rating of the borrower. If my brother-in-law had been Bill Gates of Microsoft or Steve Jobs of Apple, I would not have been so worried about his bond. In the investment world, this worry is known as credit risk or default risk. Credit ratings for bond issuers are as important as our personal credit scores. Let's see why.

What if I need my money before the maturity date of a bond? I would need to sell the loan (bond) to somebody else. For example, I could sell my brother-in-law's loan (bond) to my father and get my money back. However, my father knows my brother-in-law too well (poor credit rating), and in the old man's opinion this loan (bond) is only worth 80% of the amount of the loan. So, my father would buy this loan (bond) at a discount.

The higher the credit rating of the bond issuer, the more secure our investments are. There are several rating companies (Moody's, Standard & Poor's, etc.) that rate bonds, thus giving investors an idea of how risky a bond would be. The higher the risk, the higher the compensation we would want for letting somebody borrow our money. This compensation would come as interest payments. Let's guess from whom we would want higher interest: from Bill Gates or from my brother-in-law? My father might have agreed to pay the full amount for my brother-in-law's bond if the loan was offered at a high interest rate. In order to make higher risk debt attractive to the market, the risk must be offset by either a discounted price or a higher interest rate.

There is another risk associated with buying bonds: interest rate change risk. Bonds pay interest at a fixed rate for the entire life of the bond. This rate may appear attractive when we buy the bond. However, if the market changes to higher prevailing (current) interest rates, our older lower interest rate bond would become unattractive and worth less on the resale market. This is known as interest rate risk.

Bond prices on the resale market will vary depending on the prevailing (current) interest rates. Rising prevailing interest rates cause previously issued bonds to drop in price. Decreasing prevailing interest rates cause the price of previously issued bonds to rise. Think of a schoolyard seesaw with the market price of bonds on one side and prevailing interest rates on the other side.

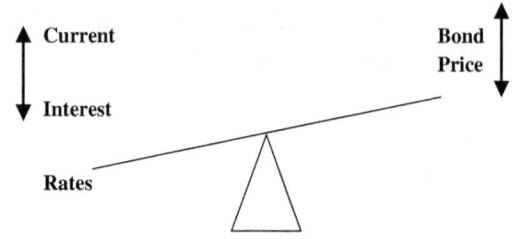

Fig.16.1 – Bond Price / Interest Rate Seesaw

The longer the maturity of the bond, the more its market price will be affected by prevailing interest rate changes. If we purchase a two-year bond and a ten-year bond both paying 5% interest and the prevailing interest rates increase to 8%, both bonds will drop in market price. However, the ten-year bond will decrease considerably more. Think of the maturity of the bond as the length of the seesaw on the bond price side of the seesaw's pivot.

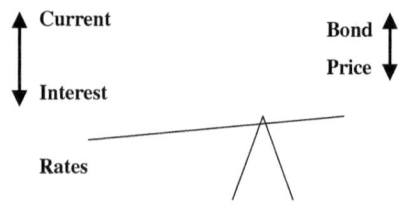

Fig.16.2 – Short Maturity
Bond Price / Interest Rate Seesaw

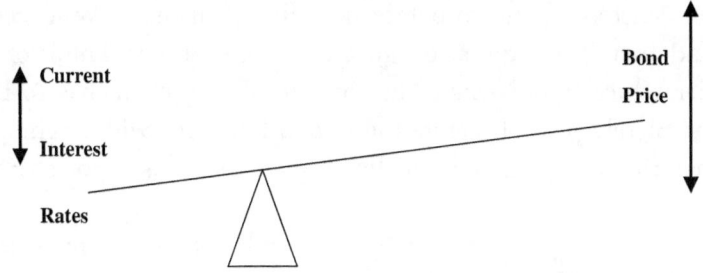

Fig.16.3 – Long Maturity
Bond Price / Interest Rate Seesaw

You may think this discussion is a waste of time because you aren't interested in buying bonds. However, most of us are already dealing with bonds on a regular basis. A certificate of deposit (CD) is a form of a bond. We are loaning money to a bank, which agrees to pay us a fixed rate of interest for a specified period of time, after which our money will be returned to us. Even a checking account is a type of a bond. When we make a deposit, we let the bank use our money for the bank's needs until withdrawal.

Corporate Bonds

When we buy a corporate bond, we are lending money to a corporation. We need to check out the bond's rating, maturity date, and interest rate to decide if a particular corporate bond is an appropriate investment for us.

Let's introduce the corporate liquidity chain here. Who gets paid first if a corporation goes into bankruptcy? Think of a hierarchical order where the top link of the chain has to be completely paid off before the second link gets paid anything, then the third, and so on. Following are the links in the chain:

> 1st Any taxes, salaries, and other immediate obligations
> 2nd Secured debt backed by named assets
> 3rd Senior bank loans
> 4th Senior bonds
> 5th Subordinate bonds
> 6th Preferred stock
> 7th Common stock

Corporate bonds can be sold in forms other than straight debt. Convertible bonds offer us an option to convert our bond to stock. Preferred stock trades like a stock but offers a higher dividend or interest payment. The name "preferred stock" is extremely misleading since these instruments behave more like bonds paying interest until maturity. Preferred shareholders do not own any equity interest in a company's good fortunes, and therefore should not be called "stocks." Preferred stock holders stand in line after *all other* bondholders in the corporate liquidity chain. They would be repaid last among bondholders but before the common stock holders. A better name for preferred stocks would be "worth less than the least secure bonds." But since it would be difficult to sell an investment vehicle with such an evocative name, someone came up with the clever name "preferred stock" instead. Don't let this name mislead you – they are the lowest quality of bonds. Although preferred stocks are the riskiest bonds, there may be circumstances that make them appropriate for some investors that understand these risks. In some circumstances, convertible preferred stocks might be suitable investments.

Treasury-Issued Bills, Notes, and Bonds

U.S. government-issued debt is considered risk-free because the U.S. government, which can print more money to repay the debt holders, backs it. So we don't have to worry about the rating, as treasury debt is not rated. Notes have maturities of two, five, or ten years. Notes and longer-term bonds pay interest every six months. Bills mature in three, six, or twelve months. Bills are issued at a discount and mature at their full face values. Their discount represents the income we receive from owning them. U.S. federal-government-issued debt is not subject to state income taxes, so their after-tax return could be higher.

An investor can also purchase "strips," for which the interest-paying part of the bond has been separated (stripped away) so that the bond only pays the face value at maturity. Strips are zero-coupon bonds bought at a deep discount to the face value that are paid at the maturity date with no interest payments in the meantime. For example, we might buy a bond for $770 knowing that in ten years we will receive $1,000. One downside to zero-coupon bonds is that the IRS assigns phantom annual income to us from owning them. We must pay taxes annually on this phantom income despite the fact we receive no actual income until the bonds mature. The second downside to zero-coupon bonds is that their prices highly fluctuate as prevailing interest rates change. Thus, if we suddenly need to sell our zero-coupon bonds, we may not get the price we expect.

In my opinion, zero-coupon bonds are gimmicks I would not recommend purchasing. They have high price volatility with taxes due on income not actually received. Corporate zero-coupon bonds are also available but are also not recommended.

Municipal Bonds

Municipal bonds are issued by local, county, state, or city governments for such projects as improving roads or educational facilities. They are backed by local and state governments and are not backed by the U.S. government. However, they tend to be safe as local municipalities can always increase our taxes to raise cash to pay us back. Note that general obligation municipal bonds tend to be safer than revenue anticipation municipal bonds. Municipal bonds are not subject to federal taxes. If we buy a bond issued by a government within the state we live, it will be exempt from state taxes as well as federal taxes.

Prepackaged Managed Investments

As you can guess, it's easier to buy stocks or bonds with large amounts of money. However, many people do not have enough money to diversify their investments with individual stocks and bonds. It's particularly difficult to diversify efficiently when we are only investing small sums monthly into our freedom accounts.

Mutual funds and other prepackaged investments can help us distribute our small monthly investments among different buckets. When we invest in a mutual fund, we are pooling our money with that of others investors, and we thus own a little portion of a bunch of different companies, instead of just one. Mutual funds can be comprised of various investments including stocks, bonds, and alternative investments. Therefore, mutual funds are as risky as the investments of which they are comprised. However, mutual funds are more diversified than individual stocks and bonds. Further, these funds are managed by teams of professionals who monitor performance and control risks.

The managers of the funds regularly make decisions on the appropriateness of investments within the funds. Different funds focus on different investment strategies. The focus could be smaller companies that are growing rapidly, or it could be large well-established companies paying high dividends. It could be stocks or bonds or a blend of both. It could be only foreign companies or only U.S. companies, or it could be both. In other words, when we buy one share of a mutual fund, we buy a tiny piece of the many diverse investments that comprise the fund.

There are four major types of funds: open-end mutual funds, closed-end mutual funds, exchange-traded funds, and unit investment trusts.

Open-End Mutual Funds
Open-end mutual funds are the most commonly known and the most advertised. Their shares are not traded on the open market. We can buy them directly from the fund companies or indirectly through brokers. The fund companies create shares as investors buy them. These shares are dissolved when investors sell them. Therefore, due to buys and sells, the pool of money the fund company manages is fluctuating and is thus open-ended.

To make things more confusing, open-end mutual funds fall into four classes: A, B, C, and no-load funds. These classes relate to how much it costs to buy and hold the fund, how much the advisor is paid for selling it, and how much it will cost to sell it when we want out.

1) Open-End A-Shares: These shares generally pay the broker/advisor a heavier upfront commission called a "load" but have a lower recurring annual expense. This front-end load (ranging from 1% to 5.75% of the invested amount paid to the broker/advisor) will reduce the money being invested in the fund. A fund with a 5% load implies that only 95 cents out of every dollar invested goes to work. These loads are typically reduced if we purchase more of a fund. Ask the broker about break points, which are purchase amounts that result in reduced loads.

The front-end load is waived if we purchase A-shares in fee-based accounts which make this share class ideal for such accounts. The load also becomes zero if we purchase more than one million dollars' worth of a fund family in a non-fee-based account.

The annual expense, often called the expense ratio, is not assessed directly to the shareholders, but it essentially reduces the annual returns of the fund. A-shares typically have the lowest expense ratios. A-class shares generally make sense for longer-term holders, (over ten years). By paying more upfront and reducing annual expenses, A-shares are generally "cheaper" than the other share classes, but we have to hold them for a longer period of time for this to be true. This makes A-shares ideal for fee-based accounts that don't pay the load but benefit from the lower expense ratio.

2) Open-End B-Shares: These shares have a heavy backend load and high annual maintenance expenses. I cannot find any practical advantage in buying these funds. Only brokers benefit from selling this class. Run from a broker who is selling you B-shares. They are never advantageous for the investor!

3) Open-End C-Shares: These shares generally carry a small upfront commission paid to the broker/advisor (about 1%) but have a higher annual expense than A-shares. Despite the 1% paid to the broker, 100% of our investment goes to work for us. This 1% fee is not charged to the client. The mutual company pays this fee hoping to recoup the cost if the investor holds the fund for a long period of time. Generally C-shares make sense for shorter-term holders, those less than six years. C-class shares are generally "cheaper" than the other share classes if held for shorter terms. These shares also carry an additional redemption charge (typically 1%) if sold within a year of the purchase date. There is no charge for selling after twelve months. It is difficult to plan to stay in an investment for over six years, the period of time that makes A-shares more economical. Therefore, I often recommend C-class funds unless we are using fee-based accounts. There is no need for C-class shares in fee-based accounts since A-class shares can be purchased without loads and have lower annual expense ratios.

4) Open-End No-Load Shares: This name *suggests* that there is no expense to an investor buying these funds. Well, if you believe in Santa Claus, the Tooth Fairy, and free lunches, then maybe you should be buying no-load funds. Do you really think that somebody would be managing, promoting, and distributing the funds for free? Do you believe that the huge no-load fund companies build their luxurious buildings without charging their customers fees? Do you believe they pay for massive advertising campaigns without charging their customers fees?

The term *no-load* is a lie! These funds *do* have expenses that are paid by someone, and that someone is the investor! They just hide their costs in higher management fees and internal transaction costs. It is true that no-load funds have no upfront fees and that there are no fees paid to a broker or advisor. However, without salesmen there are other marketing and advertising costs. In addition, there are fund maintenance and management costs that someone needs to pay. These no-load funds must also make a profit for their fund companies. They are not free! To believe otherwise is naive.

But the hidden costs of no-load funds are not the only problem. Often investors will buy these funds through "discount" brokerage houses in an attempt to save money. Since these discount firms receive nothing for selling no-load funds, they will often charge the investor a $25 service fee for such a transaction. If we are contributing $500 per month to our freedom account, these fees could become quite excessive. A $25 fee on a $500 investment equates to a 5% charge. Instead, buy C-class funds that have no upfront fee or backend fee if held more than a year.

Why should investors purchase no-load funds? I am mystified about why investors continue to make this choice. C-class shares cost very little and come with the advice of a broker. The trouble is that some investors are watching their pennies and not their dollars. They concentrate too much on commissions and end up with fewer dollars at the end of the day. It is as though they are fearful of getting professional advice on an issue critical to their future. This is looser thinking! This is the reason many people remain poor.

Closed-End Mutual Funds
Closed-end funds are very similar to open-end funds in that they have management with a strategy and a focus. However, these funds only raise money at their launch. Once the fund is launched, it is traded on an exchange like a stock. The biggest difference between open-end and closed-end funds are that closed-end funds, after they are launched, are not being promoted any more, so there are no marketing and promotional fees or charges. Their market prices are based on demand for the funds, not their asset values; therefore, sometimes we can buy them at a substantial discount to their NAV (Net Asset Value). This can be an advantage when buying, but a disadvantage when selling. Often closed-end mutual funds pay high dividends partially due to their discounts from NAV. Since no one is promoting closed-end funds, it's not easy to find good ones. Ask your broker to help you.

While open-end funds only trade at the end of a day, closed-end funds trade intra-day allowing you to buy and sell during the day at any time the market is open. We can also place limit, stop-loss, and good-to-cancel orders on closed-end funds.

Exchange-Traded Funds (ETFs)
Exchange-Traded Funds (ETFs) are generally unmanaged pools of money that are invested based on fixed criteria. They typically invest in an index or a particular sector of the market. These funds buy a group of stocks, bonds, or alternative assets, and hold them. ETFs are traded on an exchange like a stock; their prices fluctuate based on the underlying portfolio as well as changes in supply and demand for the actual ETF. However, they trade closer to their NAV than closed-end funds. The problem with ETFs is that unmanaged funds blindly follow their preset formulas and criteria. This means that if an ETF were focused on the pharmaceutical sector, they would own both the good and bad pharmaceutical stocks. I believe it is better to have an active manager who will make sure that we are investing in only the good stocks and not in the whole sector, which includes the good, the bad, and the ugly.

The investment landscape is ever-evolving and some newer ETFs are actively managed. A number of newer ETFs use selection criteria that eliminate less worthy stocks, which makes this structure acceptable. These newer actively managed ETFs deserve consideration for your portfolio. A qualified financial advisor can help identify suitable ETFs.

Exchange-Traded Notes (ETNs)
Exchange-Traded Notes (ETNs) are generally unmanaged pools of money designed to track an index or a particular sector of the market or commodity. These funds typically have less tracking error than ETFs. However, ETNs are debt securities of the firms that issue them. Thus they are subject to risk of default by the issuing firm. Lehman Brothers issued some ETNs whose

investors may be left with nothing after Lehman's bankruptcy. I only consider ETNs for short term investments where I closely follow the credit ratings of the issuing firms.

Unit Investment Trusts
Unit investment trusts are similar to ETFs, except that they are typically less liquid, have higher fees, and have preset maturity dates. Once the portfolio is selected, it is held for a fixed period of time. Unit trusts have certain tax advantages and also remain fully invested over the life of the trust. The easiest way to describe this fund is as an ETF with a maturity date, usually within five years, when the funds are automatically liquidated.

Unfortunately, there is no perfect investment out there. There are pros and cons to all of them. Talk to your investment advisor and try to find a strategy that is most appropriate for your particular situation. Go to www.poor-no-more.com for help.

Alternative Investments
Alternative investments typically seek out absolute returns versus relative returns to the stock market. Therefore, they tend to involve investments other than stocks or bonds and are not correlated to the stock and bond markets. They can make money in both up and down markets. Alternative investments can reduce the volatility of our portfolios. So, how can we invest in alternative assets?

Real Estate:
For real estate, we can invest by buying Real Estate Investment Trusts (REITs). These are publicly traded real estate companies that are traded on the stock market. Tenants-In-Common

(TIC) are privately held vehicles that allow us to invest jointly with other investors in to privately owned large properties and receive regular interest payments, plus profits when the real estate is sold. TIC can also offer huge tax deferrals. Talk to your investment advisor about them. Both REITs and TIC investments allow commercial real estate involvement without the daily management issues for the investors. Also note that we can buy ETFs and mutual funds that invest in REITs and gain greater diversification with far less money.

Hedge Funds:

For hedge funds, there is a broad array of strategies. Essentially, we are investing with a select group in a private investment partnership (these usually have a minimum ranging from $100,000 to $1,000,000). The management group typically has a substantial personal investment in the fund as well. The management uses complex strategies including shorts, derivatives, leverage, and arbitrage of distressed companies. With large amounts of cash, the hedge fund can find market irregularities with companies that have risky debt and offer to pick up this debt (in other words, bail them out) for juicy interest payments. In this case, more risk equals more reward. However, not all hedge funds are this risky. Hedge funds generally require our investment to be locked up for a year or more, so the investments are illiquid. Hedge funds are complicated and encompass a large number of strategies but can provide solid returns for the right investor. We can avoid the hedge fund minimum investment requirements by buying mutual funds that invest in them that only have a $1,000 minimum requirement.

Private Equity:
For private equity, we would pool our money with a venture capital management firm seeking to invest in small companies with potential for rapid growth. Generally, these types of investments require a significant minimum amount (often $250,000 to $1,000,000), and our money would be tied up for several years.

Commodities and Futures:
For commodities and futures, we no longer need to enter into a contract to buy or sell a specific commodity (such as oranges, corn, or pork-bellies) at a future date based on whichever direction we speculate it will go. We can instead use a more sane approach of hiring a Commodity Trading Advisor (CTA) to do the twenty-four-hour-a-day trading for us. This method typically requires a minimum $500,000 investment. For more modest means, we can pool our money into a Managed Future partnership – this typically requires a $5,000 to $50,000 minimum investment. Or we can invest in managed futures or commodity-based mutual funds that only have a $1,000 minimum.

Small individual investors have long ignored alternative investments. However, large institutions like the Yale and Harvard endowment funds have learned how important it is to include alternative investments in their portfolios. These large endowments have been steadily increasing their allocation to alternative investments. It is wise for individual investors to follow their lead.

Chapter Takeaway

Investments are complicated but not mysterious. It is best to hire a professional investment advisor to help you make the right choices, but stay personally involved. The advisor's job is to help us make choices, not make the choices for us.

C-class mutual funds are very inexpensive and offer the advantage of using the knowledge of a financial advisor. This combination is economical and is the sensible methodology for many investors. This is particularly true when making modest monthly investments into our freedom accounts. As our freedom accounts grow beyond $50,000, it is time to start mixing in some individual stocks and bonds with the help of a qualified financial advisor.

Fee-based accounts also use the knowledge of a financial advisor and are fairly inexpensive. Although fee-based accounts are subject to account minimums, these accounts offer more investment options than C-class only accounts. Since the fees are based on the value of the account, the financial advisor can only get a pay raise if the account value increases. Investors often prefer this incentive feature and find fee-based accounts as the optimal choice for them.

Finding the right financial advisor is critical. Some investment advisors promote techniques that are sub-optimal. Chapter 17 will expose some of these flawed, sub-optimal approaches and advise better strategies.

Chapter 17
Untrue Investment Truisms
Or The Effect of Aiming Too Low

Not only have our purchase-related decisions and beliefs been corrupted by self-serving outside influences, but so have our investment-related financial decisions. Although banks may invest our deposits into risky derivatives and sub-prime mortgages, their advertising to us suggests that it is unwise and unsafe to place our money with anyone but them. There are many other untrue corrupted investment beliefs implanted in our minds. Furthermore, there are many sub-optimal investment strategies that investment advisors rely on too heavily. Let's try to expose and debunk a few of them.

Untrue Truisms:
"Investing is too risky; just put your money into Certificate of Deposits (CDs) or bank savings accounts." Let's take a look at this statement from a mathematical viewpoint. Assuming we can obtain a 4.5% CD, our after-tax effective interest rate will be 2.925%. This assumes a state and federal combined tax rate of 35%. If we now subtract from this after-tax interest rate a 3% inflation rate, our after-tax and inflation interest rate is now negative. Thus, even with interest payments, our bank

savings are effectively losing purchasing power due to taxes and inflation.

The cost of absolute certainty and safety is absolute poverty.

If we don't want to be in the game, we can't complain about ending up in poverty. We must make some riskier investments to be in the gain. You must take risk to drink Champaign. Yes, a few of our investments will not work out profitably. But others will be profitable, and the net effect should be positive. I've heard people say they are unlucky when it comes to investments. However, luck has little to do with our success. If we've only had negative experiences, it may be due to our lack of knowledge about investments. Reading this book will help correct this situation.

"Seventy percent of mutual funds do not beat the S&P 500™ Index, so just invest in index funds." What an incredibly lazy statement! Even though there are many dreadful mutual funds in the market, that doesn't mean we should avoid searching for better performing funds. The statement itself suggests that thirty percent of mutual funds *do* beat the market index. Why not identify and invest in these superior funds?

Let's pause here to explain what indexes are. Keep in mind that indexes were never intended to be investment vehicles. Indexes were only intended to be tools to measure the broad market's performance. There are many indexes. The Standard & Poor's 500™ Index, one of the most popular, is comprised of the 500 largest companies. The size of a company is judged by its "market capital size" or "market cap." Market cap is defined as the total number of shares issued by a company multiplied by its current price per share. A company with 20 million shares trading at $30 a share has a 600-million-dollar market cap. As stock prices vary so do market caps, and therefore, the top 500 companies that qualify for the S&P 500™ also change. Note that the smaller market cap stocks, where we typically find the fastest growth, will not qualify for a large cap index, such as the S&P 500™.

The S&P 500™ and many other indexes are market cap-weighted indexes. This means that 500 stocks comprising the index are not equally weighted, i.e., 1/500 each, or 0.2% each of the index. The percentage weight of each stock is determined by its market cap compared to the total index's market cap. Thus, several behemoth stocks will be weighted over 1.0% of the index while hundreds of smaller companies will be weighted under 0.1%. Thus only 10 stocks often determine 20% of the index performance. As a stock's price increases, its percent weighting in the index will also increase. This market cap weighting is appropriate for an index whose goal is to track the movement of money into the markets.

However, market cap weighting is *inappropriate* for investment purposes. Remember, indexes were invented to measure the market and were never intended to be the basis of an investment strategy. Index mutual funds buy stocks comprising the index in volume matching their market cap weight in the index. If a stock price goes up, so will its market cap, and an index fund will be required to buy more shares. But this is problematic as an investment theme. It causes us to buy more of a stock as its price peaks, which is opposite to the basic premise of the market:

buy low and sell high. Market cap weighted index funds buy more as a stock becomes too high, and must sell off shares as a stock's price drops and becomes a better value investment. This is opposite to the buy low and sell high concept.

Studies have shown that if we weight the stocks on an index by almost any other method (earnings per share, growth rate, or even number of company parking spaces), the resulting index will outperform the market cap weighted index. Therefore, several funds and ETFs have been created using weighting criteria other than market cap, typically fundamentally weighted. These funds have outperformed their related indexes. Although these funds are superior to market cap weighted funds, I am not broadly recommending these fundamentally weighted funds either.

Why do some financial professionals recommend buying index funds? I see two basic causes for these inferior recommendations: laziness and fear of liability. With the invention of personal computers and low-cost tax software, CPAs have been challenged with replacing lost income from clients doing their own taxes. Some have replaced this lost income by providing investment advice to their clients. Since these professionals are not dedicated full-time to investment advice, they do not have the time, knowledge, or inclination to do the research. They instead stick with the easy path of recommending index mutual funds. Shame on them!

Advisors' other justification for recommending index mutual funds is to limit their perceived liability. If they recommend an index that equates to how most people measure the market (the

S&P 500™), then it becomes impossible to under-perform the market. Thus, they can blame any negative return on what the "market" did and not their recommendations. The important flip side to this argument is that it is also impossible to outperform the market. Matching the market's performance should never be anyone's goal. Having good investment returns in both bad and good market conditions is the appropriate goal.

Most portfolio managers judge their performance on a relative basis versus some index such as the S&P 500™. I strongly suggest we abandon reviewing our portfolios on a relative basis. Instead, judge performance on an absolute basis – monitor performance without regard to how an index performed. Funds that tend to seek absolute returns typically perform better in negative markets.

"Using modern portfolio theory and the efficient frontier, we can optimize our portfolios with a computer algorithm." Wow! I wish it were this simple. The efficient frontier concept *does have merit*. However, it also has a major flaw: it relies too much on prior performance being similar to future performance. This typically does not happen in real life. The law recognizes this by requiring all investment performance statements to include an advisory stating, "Past performance does not guarantee future results." Sound familiar? My advice is to run from nerdy investment advisors who rely too heavily on their flawed efficient frontier computer algorithms.

By now I'm sure many of you are asking, "What the heck is the efficient frontier?" Let me explain this with an example. Let's say we are conservative investors who only invested in bonds in order to minimize risk and volatility. However, bonds do carry some risk, and even a diversified bond portfolio will see some volatility. The efficient frontier concept argues that blending some stocks into a pure bond portfolio results in enhanced returns and less volatility.

How is this possible? First, the efficient frontier concept uses the assumption (from past performance data) that stocks' average performance is greater than bonds' average performance; therefore, the blended return will be greater than a bond-only portfolio.

Second, the efficient frontier concept uses the assumption (from past data) that there is a low correlation between stocks and bonds. Therefore, blending stocks and bonds in the optimum proportion will result in lower volatility than either stocks or bonds alone.

What is correlation? The correlation factor is a number between "+1" and "−1" that indicates how much stocks and bonds traditionally move relative to each other. A correlation factor of "+1" would indicate that stocks and bonds move together. If stocks moved up 10%, we would expect bonds to also move up exactly the same, 10%. A correlation factor of "0" indicates that their movements are completely unrelated to each other. A correlation factor of "-1" indicates that their movements are completely opposite of each other – if one goes up 10%, the other should go down 10%. This is called perfectly negative correlation.

If we assume a fixed correlation, it is possible to calculate the exact blend of the two investments that will result in minimum volatility and risk. The problem is that the correlation number is an *assumption* based on historical relative movements in the two investments. The correlation number will be different if we use historic movements from the past three years versus the last twenty to determine the correlation. Which numbers best determine the future: numbers from the past twenty years or numbers from the last three years? This depends on how market conditions are changing. Further, it's also possible that past performance has no predictive indication of future events. In this case, the whole efficient frontier concept has no merit. The bottom line is that unless someone has a crystal ball that accurately predicts the future, the efficient frontier concept is no better than the assumption used in making the calculation. It can be a useful tool, but it should not be the only tool we use to compose our investment portfolio.

The efficient frontier is a good starting point to know what would have been optimal in the past. From this starting point the financial advisor is in a position to make decisions about future strategies. We should hire skilled investment managers to actively adjust our portfolios into the best asset classes. Further, I believe that active portfolio managers' predictive abilities can far outperform a fixed computer-generated scheme based on historical data. In short, look forward, and ignore the advice of computer nerds who *only* look backwards.

"By asset allocating across all nine style boxes we can avoid much of the market volatility." Wow! Again, I wish it were this simple. This practice is just a lazy, sub-optimum method for constructing a portfolio. Although this strategy had some merit in the eighties and nineties, when growth and value portfolios had lower correlation, it has much less merit in the modern world, where growth and value are very correlated, i.e., correlation higher than 0.85. In today's market, such a simplistic strategy results in an under-performing, highly volatile portfolio.

Okay, I'm sure you are now asking, "What the heck are the nine style boxes?" Most stock mutual funds invest using either a growth or value investment theme. Growth funds seek out stocks with earnings and price growth momentum, assuming their upward momentum will continue. Value funds seek out stocks with prices that appear too low compared to their earnings potential – stocks that are currently being ignored by the markets. In past markets, blending growth and value portfolios tended to reduce volatility due to their low correlation. Some funds would blend both growth and value themes and call themselves a blended portfolio.

Funds may also specialize in the size of companies they invest in. These would include large-cap, mid-cap, and small-cap specializations. By combining the possible investment themes and the three company size specializations, nine total styles are created. The nine style boxes are shown below.

The Nine "Stock" Style Boxes

Value Blend Growth

			Large-Cap
			Mid-Cap
			Small-Cap

Similarly, nine style boxes exist for bond portfolios. In this case, we consider three maturity themes (periods): long, intermediate, and short. In each of these themes, we then consider three different qualities of bonds to obtain the nine style boxes.

The Nine "Bond" Style Boxes

Short Intermediate Long

			High Quality
			Medium Quality
			Low Quality

Again, I go back to the issue of fixed allocation being suboptimal and lazy. Why fix our allocation among these style boxes? Is it not better to predict which box will perform better in the short term and actively overweight our investments in that appropriate style box?

This brings up the issue of investment timing. Often I've heard investment professionals state that no one can time the market. Timing the market means having the ability to foresee which sectors of the market will perform better in the short run. It means predicting which sectors to avoid and which sectors to overweight when managing an investment portfolio. From a statistical perspective, these advisors have a point. The *average* mutual fund seeking to time the market may not outperform the index. Therefore, some advisors often prefer a fixed asset allocation. But why settle for average? Shouldn't our aim be higher?

Many mutual fund managers are not adept at timing the market. However, a few exceptional managers can. Timing the market is an obtainable goal for some premium managers. We should hire skilled investment managers with track records of predicting which style boxes to overweight. The results should be much better than sticking money into all nine style boxes and burying our heads in the sand. In short, a stagnant allocation results in stagnant performance, while dynamic allocation can result in dynamic performance.

"Diversification is the key to investment performance and safety." I agree with this statement more than any of the other truisms. Although diversification is necessary, it is not sufficient by itself to provide either superior performance or safety. Many professionals rely too heavily on diversification. The quality of the managers selected, the quality of the individual investments selected, and the correlation between these selections is what provides both performance and safety.

Diversification has diminishing effects. Too much diversification becomes what I call "deworsesification." With too much diversification, it becomes impossible to outperform the market, because our portfolio covers so many sectors that it mimics the market. Providing our portfolio managers with the freedom to pick and choose sectors gives them the ability to outperform the broader market.

"Asset allocation across all sectors is important for both performance and safety." Asset allocation is important, but we shouldn't put a manager in jail for going out on a limb. Managers should be free to have zero investment in some sectors and significant concentrations in other sectors. This is why we hire them, to make decisions on which sectors to avoid and which sectors to load up on.

Some investment advisors recommend that portfolios should be allocated among *all* sectors. This is equivalent to betting on all ten horses to win a race. Sure, we are guaranteed to pick a winner, but we are also guaranteed to have nine losers. Again, allocating to everything is "deworsesification."

"Using classical automatic rebalancing fixed asset allocation is the only responsible way to invest." This concept is not a commitment to excellence but instead a commitment to

mediocrity. To embrace this concept means we must also embrace its assumptions, which include: a skilled portfolio manager can't time the market; a skilled portfolio manager's security or sector decisions do not matter; and it's better to have automatic allocation rebalancing instead of a skilled portfolio manager deciding when it is time to rebalance.

Automatic rebalancing means periodically trimming money from the better performing investments and reallocating the proceeds to the worse performing investments. When an investment advisor suggests automatic rebalancing, a bell should go off in our heads. This ringing bell is an indication that this advisor is going to spend very little time personally reviewing our portfolio to determine when changes should be made. Should we prefer an involved concerned investment advisor or a simple calendar-based computer program to make our investment decisions? Further, we need to let our winners keep running until they run out of gas. Would it have been right to trim Microsoft or Apple after their first two years?

Recommended Investment Strategies:

I have talked about what I don't like. What do I like? Well, for higher-net-worth folks, individual stocks and bonds with active management are typically best. However, most folks will not have enough money to properly diversify with individual securities. So mutual funds are the right answer for most people.

Which mutual funds are the best? Well, this depends on the investors' individual goals, expectations, risk tolerance, and stage of life. An older conservative person dependent on interest income has different needs than someone just getting started. For these older folks, there are many types of income-producing mutual funds, many of which do not include bonds. Contact the people at www.poor-no-more.com for help finding appropriate investment advisors.

For younger, more growth-oriented investors, I prefer team-based portfolio managers with wide-open charters covering all sectors that have a proven long-term track record. What I am referring to here is mutual funds that meet three important criteria:

1) Team-based manager with a well-defined investment process.
2) Wide-open charters allowing all types of investments.
3) Proven track record.

Teams

Don't rely too much on an individual manager. The fund should have a team approach so that if something happens to an individual manager, the team could replace the individual without disturbing the fund's performance. The investment selection process should be a well-defined process used by all the members of the team. Relying on a selection process instead of relying on one individual's judgment is the key. Losing one team member should not affect the process. Relying too much on a single individual's judgment makes the future performance of the fund subject to that individual. Better to have a team with a strategy and process that can be passed down.

Wide-Open Charters

The charter limits what types of investments a mutual fund may own. Some investment advisors prefer to invest in each of the style boxes by selecting managers narrowly focused in each style box or in each sector, e.g., small-cap value technology. There is some merit to this since a narrowly focused manager could do a better job in a single sector. However, in today's rapidly changing environment, I believe a predetermined allocation is dangerous and sub-optimal. We need to give managers the freedom to rapidly change from sector to sector as market conditions change.

Wide-open charter mutual funds are often called asset allocation funds. However, not all asset allocation mutual funds are created equal. Some funds in this classification have a fixed allocation. This is **NOT** what we want! We want a mutual fund charter that allows the manager to actively move between growth and value and to move among small-cap, mid-cap, and large-cap. Further, the manager should be able to freely select between domestic and international investments or between stocks and bonds. We want funds that allow managers to select and over-concentrate in certain sectors at certain times while avoiding other sectors. We want funds that allow managers to find returns wherever they may exist.

Other wide-open charter freedoms should include the right to go short, the right to hedge, and the right to invest in alternative investments including commodities and currency exchanges. Shorting is a technique that profits when a stock declines in price. Hedging is a form of investment insurance protecting us from unanticipated market movements. Commodity and Currency exchanges are a huge part of the financial markets often ignored by smaller investors. The more tools (or investment types) our managers have, the better the opportunity to outperform the market.

Track Record

Even if fund managers had all the flexibility in the world, that flexibility is worthless if they don't know how to take advantage of it. The only proof of their knowledge is their performance record. Morningstar.com is a great place to compare mutual fund performance figures. I would completely ignore the one-year performance record. Further, I would place little emphasis on Morningstar's "star ratings." Instead, I would emphasize and compare three-, five-, and ten-year performance records. Morningstar also provides annual performance during each of the past ten years. Examine a fund's performance year by year against the index and get a feeling for how the fund performed in bad years. I like to place more emphasis on how a fund performed during bad market years. The upside/downside capture ratio is another way to examine how mutual funds did in various market conditions.

How do we construct a portfolio? In short, I believe that instead of trying to allocate across various sectors, we should allocate across various fund managers who then allocate dynamically across sectors as allowed by their wide-open charters. However, there are many other valid strategies that I encourage and recommend to my clients. Some are quite complicated and beyond the scope of this book. It is important for investors to work with qualified investment advisors who understand their clients' needs and can implement appropriate strategies. Contact the people at www.poor-no-more.com for help finding the suitable investment advisors.

Chapter Takeaway

Constructing an optimal investment portfolio is not simple. It cannot be done with computer algorithms and fixed asset allocations. Our portfolios must be dynamically flexible to match today's dynamically changing markets conditions. This means there must be professional advisors helping us make complex decisions about the future.

How do we find such appropriate advisors? The financial advisor selection process is the key. Avoid advisors who over-concentrate on the imperfect flawed strategies I previously talked about in this chapter. Remember that these flawed strategies are often presented in such a way that they sound foolproof – they are not. Avoid advisors that have limited experience. An appropriate advisor should have at least ten years in the business or be working in a team with more experienced members. An advisor should have proven his ability to study and learn. Therefore, we should reject advisors who have not obtained a college degree. In addition, a Certified Financial Planner™ designation demonstrates an advisor's dedication to provide professional services to his clients.

How about licensing and registration? Don't take investment advice from agents who only have an insurance license. Although they may call themselves financial advisors, obviously their advice will only include insurance-based solutions. Only take advice from financial advisors who have both their insurance license and Series 7 (stock broker's license). We need advisors who can recommend all types of solutions when they are appropriate. Avoid advisors who only have a Series 6 license. The Series 6 license is very limited, only allowing for mutual fund sales. Advisors with only Series 6 licenses are either not interested in providing full service or lack the intellect to pass the much more rigorous Series 7 exam. Only select advisors who are dedicated enough to the business to complete both their Series 7 and insurance licensing.

Does it matter which firm the advisor works for? The answer is not really. What matters is the individual advisor. However, be careful not to select a firm or advisor that pushes the firm's proprietary products. Run from an advisor working for company XYZ whose solutions involve XYZ's branded product.

Once again, there is a significant difference between how wealthy people and poor people think. Wealthy people get advice from qualified financial professionals. Poor people get advice from quacks, or their poor friends, or try to do it themselves. Again, contact the people at www.poor-no-more.com for help finding appropriate investment advisors.

Chapter 18
Wrapping It All Up

The purpose of this book has been to give you a roadmap, with concrete steps, on how to achieve financial freedom. In order to do this, we needed to examine our belief systems and question many of our long-held notions of how things should be done.

We can never be wealthy if we still think like poor people.

We talked about how outside influences, like Madison Avenue, can lead us to do things that are not in our best interest and that can stand in the way of achieving our quest for financial freedom. We need to reject our previous beliefs about money and learn to make decisions the way wealthy people make decisions.

We examined traditional retirement beliefs and concluded that traditional retirement is an obsolete concept. Instead of savings for retirement, we should save for financial independence in the near term by building our freedom accounts.

It's easier to place money in a freedom account that we can benefit from next year than a classic retirement account with benefits decades away!

The freedom account concept is this book, shows how we can achieve financial freedom sooner than we think. Instead of saving for a time decades away, we can use the freedom account to obtain financial gratification in the near term. This allows us to take more chances in choosing a more satisfying and rewarding career path. We become less dependent on our paychecks and can feel financial serenity sooner.

Once we neutralize the outside forces trying to get us to buy whatever they are selling, we gain more control over out financial lives. We differentiate "wants" from "needs" and we improve our lifestyle by eliminating wasteful spending. This enables us to get to the business of funding our freedom accounts.

We must realize that a war is being waged to control our minds and purchase decisions.

We discussed how destructive debt can be to our financial well-being. We determined what is the proper use of credit and debt, and what is not. We learned how our credit score is determined and what we can do to improve our scores, which will reduce our interest costs.

We reviewed methods of buying houses, cars, and other necessities that propel us towards our goal instead of presenting unnecessary obstacles that can ruin our ultimate success in achieving financial freedom.

We examined the world of investments. We challenged common misconceptions. We learned to better understand the nature of different investments and which ones can be beneficial to achieving our goals. We also talked about investments that have dangerous or negative features.

Finally, we outlined what we need to look for when we seek financial advice. We examined the characteristics of financial advisors who have our interest at heart. We also learned how to recognize and select financial advisors that are not just out for themselves.

The more you snooze the more you lose!

The most important thing is to get moving on the concepts from this book. The sooner you start on these techniques, the bigger the difference will be and the more fulfilling your life will be. Doing nothing, or delaying getting started, is a decision. It's the wrong decision! Get going in making you life and the lives of your loved ones better. Again, contact the people at www.poor-no-more.com for help in finding an appropriate financial advisor that can help you get started.

Thanks for listening!

www.ingramcontent.com/pod-product-compliance
Lightning Source LLC
Chambersburg PA
CBHW071415170526
45165CB00001B/289